FROM THIS MOMENT . . .

Edited by Bobby Tobolik

First published in Great Britain in 2005 by
POETRY NOW
Remus House,
Coltsfoot Drive,
Peterborough, PE2 9JX
Telephone (01733) 898101
Fax (01733) 313524

SB ISBN 1 84602 011 5

FOREWORD

Although we are a nation of poets we are accused of not reading poetry, or buying poetry books. After many years of listening to the incessant gripes of poetry publishers, I can only assume that the books they publish, in general, are books that most people do not want to read.

Poetry should not be obscure, introverted, and as cryptic as a crossword puzzle: it is the poet's duty to reach out and embrace the world.

The world owes the poet nothing and we should not be expected to dig and delve into a rambling discourse searching for some inner meaning.

The reason we write poetry (and almost all of us do) is because we want to communicate: an ideal; an idea; or a specific feeling. Poetry is as essential in communication, as a letter; a radio; a telephone, and the main criterion for selecting the poems in this anthology is very simple: they communicate.

CONTENTS

THE ANGUISH

Grey, fatigued, and careworn faces,
After all those years of war.
They joined up as boys, but now were men,
They will never find their youth again.
Losing comrades, such heartache,
But having to do your duty,
The daily grind, all this strife,
Knowing you could lose your life.
Now we are told there's something on,
Maybe something to end this war.
There is going to be another push,
But up to now it's all 'hush-hush'.
Now it's here, they call it D-Day,
We're going to reach those beaches.
Whatever it costs, we're going to land,
And try our best to take command.
All those soldiers with tired faces,
Ready to take their chances,
Small boats, big boats, anything that goes,
We're going head on to meet the foes.
Now we are approaching Normandy,
They are shelling all around.
Whoops! Another one, 'Charlie' is no more,
And we haven't actually reached the shore.
Another shell, I feel the pain,
And I've just stood on the beach.
I'm in hospital when I come round,
And my feet had only touched the ground.
I know this landing will be a success,
And help to end this war,
I know that good sense will prevail,
I also know we can't fail!

Edith Antrobus

FOR JERRY
(In memory of the great composer Jerry Goldsmith)

Patient, gently melodic waves
Of aching, rising splendour
Stir obedient, untouched depths
Into gradual, lyrical momentum . . .

Cosmos as a canvas of hope,
The Enterprise his daring strokes
In recklessly inventive phrasing:
This Star composer's musical Trek.

. . . A slow-wound fuse of adrenaline,
Usurper of my panicked heart blood,
At the reigns of runaway rhythm
In gallop to magisterial heights . . .

An aching, filial lullaby
For a tragic omen of evil;
Possessing childhood as malice
In torrential Satanic chorus.

. . . The march of thunderous percussion:
Unperturbed 'neath flammable hail
'Til a final, explosive cadence
Erupts its full orchestral force.

Robert Appleton

UNTITLED

At night I prayed
And was told the morn
Again in words delayed
Would realise my urgent
Words for the dawn
And yet again resurgent
My words reborn
Sent their fire lent
At times in personal despair
At other times yet torn
Answers and revelation rare
Could in truth be told.
Now many years have past and born
Along the roads of time a memory
        recurs of long-past hopes of old.

John Amsden

WHY?

I'm fighting this war, but I don't know why
You discharge bullets, fight or die
The enemies are there, they multiply
I remember my training, you laugh or cry
The orders I'm told, I shoot and comply
But the horrors of war magnify
Once shot you're a squashed mince pie
I should have been, my own private eye
We're under attack, the missiles let fly
I utter a prayer, a silent goodbye
My stomach hurts, there's a pain in my thigh
Some bodies are charred and even deep fried
I flew here by plane to the countryside
But wander round dazed, so starry-eyed
My skin is like leather and sun-dried
You see corpses side by side
In death were still, unoccupied
People think fighting is an easy ride
Tit for tat but we're all dog tired
See through my eyes, you'd be horrified
Is all of this killing justified?

A Allen

SHE

She captivates me with her smile and
Intoxicates me with her spirit
She's all that my eyes can see and
My heart longs for her every minute.

P Allinson

WHITE

White veil across a bridal face,
Dress of satin, trimmed with lace,
White swans gliding on the lake,
Icing on the Christmas cake,
Long white beard - Santa Claus,
Snow White and the seven dwarfs,
White sails billow in the breeze,
Foaming surf of crashing seas,
Crisp white sheets and shirts so fine,
Blowing on the linen line,
White-capped mountains, little white lies,
Clouds and angels dance in the skies
Haunting ghosts appear at night,
Saw one once - went white with fright,
Whose footprints are those in the snow?
Abominable snowman - no one knows,
White pearls that ladies love to wear,
North Pole, icebergs, polar bear,
White water rapids in a rush,
Toothpaste slides along the brush,
Your teeth are really pearly white,
Snowflakes softly fall at night,
White Cliffs of Dover - they all sang,
Cream atop a white meringue,
Lace shawl wrapped around a babe,
White lilies for your loved one's grave,
Blossom on the trees above,
Peace on Earth - a pure white dove,
Some colours - well they are all right,
But I love these 'cause they're all white!

Hilary Ambrose

WORDS

Words of beauty,
Words of pain,
Words like gentle summer rain.
Words that softly ease the mind
Words of caring,
Words of kind.

They fill your heart
And steal your soul,
Can break you down or make you whole.
Go carefully with what you say,
For words can make or break the day.

L Arnold

Soz

I'm, you know, you know what I mean, you know what I want to say
You know, for what I did to you, you know, the other day

I wasn't myself, don't know what came over me
Took me a while to realise, took me this long to see

Didn't mean it to come out that way, didn't mean what I said
You know how things can be, the fire's started and all you see is red

I hope that you can find it in your heart to forgive me
Once I was blind, but now I can see

I am *sorry*

Bisi Akinola-Arutoghor

DAISIES

Galaxies of daisies
On the spacious lawn,
Terra firma firmament
Dimly green at dawn.
Now the sun has risen
Stars so brightly show,
Twinkling, clust'ring at my feet,
Heaven here below.

Magical white dream dust
By a wizard sown
Now has grown up all haphazard
And soon must be mown.
Dear flowers, I cannot spare you
Though I do regret
I must tread your milky way
And you decapitate.

Because I know your nature
I do not grieve too sore;
New, valiant little heads
You'll raise, and shine once more.
So when life lays me low
And I feel distress or pain
Oh may God grant me strength and faith
To live and hope again.

V M Archer

LOST FRIENDSHIP

I'd like to dedicate this verse to someone I adored,
A friend who was so very dear, who never was ignored.
So many other friends would come and go with so much ease,
But Rhian, she was always there, no need to ask her please.

But sadly she has passed away some several years ago,
A very special angel in the afterlife I know,
Her memory will always stay within my heart it's true,
Someone that will not be forgotten, whatever I will do.

My life was filled with sadness and she's left an empty space,
No one I know will ever be the one to take her place,
But life goes on I realise, she'll never be forgot,
I feel her spirit all around but happy I am not.

I miss the company she gave when she was by my side,
And if she was not happy, yes her feelings she could not hide,
But yes, we were so close you know and this I miss so much,
That she's not here to be my friend, I cannot feel her touch.

So rest in peace my precious friend until again we meet,
Although I'm sad that you're not here my heart is incomplete,
Your life was cut so very short, so cruel and unkind,
No one will ever fill your shoes, no better friend I'll find.

So sad I lost your friendship.

Robert Basham

LIFTED HIGH

Easter time and all is new,
God sent His only Son for you
So when you see Him lifted high
Underneath that dark grey sky
You will know the reason why
Christ on Earth He had to die.

S Bannister

A Moment In Time

Life is just a moment,
And then it is gone.
Why, live for every second,
Then contentment is life's bond!

No time to look back
At life gone by.
It's how you put it right,
Not to sit and cry!

Learn by your mistakes,
For we're all finding our way.
Also by helping others,
Adds value to your day!

Then treasure magical moments,
There're pictures in your mind.
With emotions and feelings,
No man can ever define!

So one learns to treasure
All these moments in time.
As it gives one strength,
When life's on the decline!

Ann Beard

MONUMENTS IN STONE

Lest we forget we build monuments in stone
A thousand strangers' names, others loved and known
Battles both won and lost, for centuries gone past
With each great war we're promised, this will be the last
Mothers are relieved, thinking their sons are safe from war
Truth is no one can know, what the future has in store
We think a lesson's been learnt, from mistakes of the past
History tells another story, peace never lasts
And so we continue building monuments in stone
Whilst sending mothers' sons to war, for reasons unknown
Where they simply follow orders of others in command
Who in turn carry out those issued, in some far-off homeland
Where silver-tongued politicians use their spin like charms
To persuade young men to sally forth and take up lethal arms
So yet another generation's young men march off to war
Just like the many thousands have all those times before
Proudly with heads held high and their stance erect
Whilst we continue building monuments, lest by chance, we forget

Beverley Balogh

REMEMBER ME

Please don't cry, my friends, I'm not that far away,
And if you really need me, then all you need do is pray.
For your prayer will reach me and your words of love I'll hear,
So please remember I love you so and your love remains with me here.
I know I had to go away, so sudden it may have been,
But I have to say I thank you for it was on you, you let me lean.
Never forget me please I beg this of you
For your love for me was so very strong and true.
There may be times you'll see me, in some sweet memory,
And all I ever ask of you, is just remember me.

M Barrow

EASTER

Easter eggs for sale so many,
yellow bows on Easter bunnies.
Roast lamb with mint,
upon warm plate.
Hot cross buns and chocolate cake.

Time off work to chill and see
new creation, flower and tree.
Warmth of sun
to shine and give
new hope to life, the will to live.

Remember Him, who gave Himself.
All creation suffers loss,
not our Lord upon His cross.
He rose again. The price is paid
man and God's new fragrant place.

D Brooks

ONE GOD

One 'God' but one in every one of us,
Depending on what we allow in,
How much outside is taken inside,
How much inside is allowed to show.
And 'God' is what is you,
Friend or foe, good or evil,
But generally a mixture of the two,
Helping and hurting: You!
You are not a few genes flung together
Nor specifically designed.
It's not the colour of your hair or eyes
Or size of your feet, nose or shoulders.
It's you and the way you reason.
'God' in you is not facts absorbed, useless knowledge.
'God' in you is wisdom and the ability to care.
Whatever inside you, you allow in
Is part of the wisdom that makes 'God',
Good or evil. 'God' is all around and part of you.
'God' can only be if he exists and is perfection,
For 'God' has to be the ultimate to be 'God'.
And only can 'God' be if he is total part of his own creation
So only can 'God' exist as a natural force,
A cloud, the wind, a storm, the sun,
The rain, the falling leaves, a flower,
A shell, the sea, the sand and me and you.

Joan E Blissett

D-DAY, 60 YEARS ON

We who were the youth of yesteryear
Now are old - but some at least still here.
Are we the lucky ones who live to grow old,
Or are those who never lost their youth - whose song was left untold?
We cannot tell and who will care?
Those who chanced all and are no longer here?
Life is a gamble - life is a chance,
Some lives a burden - others just live to dance.
But what is important is, we learn by our mistakes,
Often in life there's much to bear - with only a few lucky breaks.
Age brings experience and that's what we all need,
With families to bring up and hungry children to feed.
Youth can't always find something that experience can supply,
And for once, youth - on age - can often rely.
Leave a little wisdom behind you,
Give help and a little kindness too,
Then perhaps, my friend, you'll not have lived a life that was in vain,
And sunshine will surely filter through the storms of life and rain.

J Bartlett

PAPER PASSION

I miss you dear friend, I miss you
When will you return
So once more I may kiss you?
The strength of your fingers
With me still lingers
The warm beat of your heart
Keeps time with mine.

Dear friend I miss you, I miss you
And long, oh so long for to kiss you
The jut of your chin
The fall of your hair
The slight slanting grin
That tells me you care
The grasp of your hand
The clasp of your tie,
The yearning to see you
Before another year goes by.

Your heart in my bosom will lie
Still and close until the day I die
Our love is forbidden, we both know this
But it's alright on paper
With a paper kiss.

Marie Brown

UNDERSTAND ME

Please don't misunderstand me,
I am not what you think a maniac,
I am a person of a distinctive character,
Maybe born between the lunar month,
My life is just a nice one,
You can describe it as like a prism,
I am not a specialist,
We all wish we have that special characteristic,
Of a special person,
But my life is really a simple one,
I believe in eternal love,
I believe in the eternal light,
Please understand me,
And my simple ways,
I believe in God.

A Bhambra

OLD MOTHER ENGLAND

A picture postcard hamlet
with walls of honeyed stone
and kitchen-garden hollyhocks
that harbour round their home
is now forever England -
so peaceful and serene
with lavender and honeysuckle,
vibrant village green . . .

Old timber-framed thatched cottages
and alpine plants that thrive,
nasturtiums and clematis,
a topiary-hive
becomes the perfect complement
to aviary and stocks
a path of random stepping stones
with seat of rustic blocks . . .

The cricket feuds and bonfire nights
of golden autumn days
and timeless English customs
that are blended in the haze
golden as a metaphor -
Idyllic summer breeze
and cherry blossom glimpsing
through umbelliferous trees . . .

Kenneth Berry

INSIDE OUT

I gaze from within me
upon the outside.
A shell, a soft shell,
filled with feelings, memories, yearnings.
I peer beyond.
I see not behind,
save I turn,
and whatever,
is gone.

Diane Bowen

THUNDER IN THE SKIES

Thunder in the skies
And the Lord
Glanced down from Heaven
With lightning in His eyes.
And God's Holy Spirit
Moves with the power
Like thunder in the skies.

David A Bray

SHIFTING SANDS

Stop what you're doing
I don't agree with what you're saying

You're too possessive,
Too demanding of my time.

Sometimes I have to say no for my own good,
For my own peace of mind.

You call that cruel,
I call it self-preservation.

Opposites no longer attract.
Chalk 'n' cheese does not taste good,
Where is equality? Where is balance?

But there will be no arguments,
Just a strategic withdrawal.

Your tales of woe weary me,
Your lack of insight disappoints me,
Always down, always down.

My bonds are beginning to loosen,
I can't do this anymore.

Something is not quite right
I feel I'm being manipulated

I may be wrong, but that's how I feel,
We're sinking in shifting sand.

Ian Bosker

MARSEILLES

You were there
back in the hazy days.
I recall the aura.
Swimming like fish
in clear warm seas.
It is warmth around me
with colours blurred and flashing
and smiling faces everywhere.

Come home to where I am.

The seaweed greens
where we swam,
laughed and screamed too
because the vivid reality
was so hard to take.

There the blue of summer skies
and somewhere, the lilac.

M Braithwaite

SPRING - AGAIN!

Every possible thing
Has been said about spring.
What can I say more
When great bards went before?
She 'goeth all in white'
And lambs skip with delight.
New blossoms appear;
It's a season held dear.
The sun makes flowers grow;
All poets say so.
The weather is fine,
The air is like wine,
So
Get out and imbibe it,
Don't stay to describe it!

Carol Burton

IS GOD REAL TO YOU?

There is this person, that people believe,
Where others less willing, cannot conceive,
No one has seen Him or heard His voice,
Their own belief, a given choice,
There's nowhere to hide, without His knowing,
No outward signs, no trumpet blowing,
You can kneel or sit, lay or stand,
They do it in silence or with a brass band,
It's not what you say, it's more what you do,
Posing this question, 'Is God real to you?'

Graham Burns

SOMEONE SPECIAL

We moan about wrinkles and growing old.
We complain that the weather's too hot or too cold.
Have you ever had a thought to spare,
For those who have much more to bear?

Someone very special who touched my soul,
Brave and courageous for whom life's bell did toll,
Undaunted by illness and illuminated from within,
Gutsy and spunky, never once giving in.

Wise beyond his years, that set him apart,
With astute sensitivity he melted my heart,
Living each new day with quiet acclaim,
He really put us all to shame.

Linda Bruce

THE CHOCOLATE BOX

The battle for the last chocolate in the box
Began with some small talk
About how the last was bound to be the worst
Then slowly built from, 'Well if you don't want it', to, 'You ate most',
And ended with a list of dietary indiscretions and overweight jokes.

Robert Black

ON THE MARGINS

He builds His church
On the margins of society
With people often distasteful
To you and me,
Fully aware of their sin hidden
Deep within.
God scans with His eyes
The Sunday pew
With the comfortable few
Who pray and go away
Satisfied their duty is done,
For they have glorified the Son.
As they kneel and pray
Will they not hear the Lord say,
On your way out feel and identify
With the raw reality of the marginalised
This and every day,
Till the heart sings
Of the glory of the King of Kings
With true humility?

P D Bidmead

DISCOVERIES

The day I discovered your mouth with its open secret
I discovered myself, dawn entered all the windows.
You turned a petalled darkness inside my chest,
Set a fixed place no waters can shake or move.

Your steps like sleep came stirring among my grasses,
Before night spoke, before the house built of silence
Entered to name you, echoed back one known voice.
I waited as none since waited to focus the mirror's dance.

Discoveries wait on words; but my heart is open,
And memories shape white hands to the chaliced lip;
Across my brows you bend a dark wing of shadows,
Blowing the fuse of time with your fingertips.

The day I discovered your heart with its birds of morning,
New singing landscapes tuned a taut string gone slack,
Nothing from now can loosen, or snap the music,
Only time's waves unnoticed turn brokenly in and back.

Alan C Brown

ANGUISH

Lamps sparkled like jewels adorning the coast,
in the fast fading evening light;
but the pleasure it gave me just wasn't the same
as the joy of the previous night.

We'd sat on the pier while a gentle sea breeze
caressed us and ruffled our hair:
reflections were etched in the wet golden sand,
and music was in the night air.

We parted in haste - you ran for the bus,
and here was the sting, sad to say;
for while I stood waving, that same gentle breeze
just took your phone number away.

Jonathan Bryant

MIRROR ME

(Dedicated to Jesus)

How can my heart convey the joy
This man has given me.

My eyes that once were tightly shut
He opened, so I may see.

May see Him as He truly is
I sing my praise to Thee
He lets me know, all I behold
Could also mirror me.

Just as Him to illumine you
Your dark and desolate way
Open to Him, the door to your heart
And forever He will stay.

This man will take such care of your love
Your love He will not abuse
Be the keeper of your heart?

This man will not refuse.

Once inside, you will feel His love
He's everywhere you see
He lets me know, all I behold
Could also mirror me.

Lindsey Susan Powell

WATER-COLOURED PAINTING

Travel with me
along this mind image
one created from despair
seen through eyes
that have been swollen
for many a year
life was cruel
fate dealt the worst
hand of poker
and the moon
turned black on
the day she was born.
Death began to
seem beautiful
that night she knew
was her last
laying her bruised
human form
in the warm water
bathing in her own
negativity, she cut
through main wrist veins
euphoria took
the place of pain
she lay in a crimson
water-coloured painting
of her own death.

Karen Canning

DOLPHINS IN A LANDSCAPE

Dolphins weave a thread of satin through soft water
with a private purpose that we cannot fathom.
The sea is smooth and warm, impenetrable, dark.
Over the straits the mountains rise rank after rank
and fade towards a kind of stepped infinity.
There is a wonder in the air, as at a birth . . .

Oh, the bliss, the surging ache to lie together
in contemplation of possible perfection!
Through tight closed eyes we see the blue sky, the gilded
flecks of foam dancing on the innocuous waves,
listen to their riches spilling over the rocks,
the golden green fields singing across the sea.
Untarnished happiness and love, infinite joy -
all are created in this tiny space, lasting
for this richest moment that will not come again.

David C Taylor

PAIN A GAIN

Want not sacrifice
Won't not pay the price -
Lost no more
Lose no more.

Gain complain:
Gain gains pain!
Want no a gain
Want shot; refrain.

Pain swallow; decease
Want we show peace
So cease!
Slow cease.

Before we cease the pain.

Kiran Kaur Rana

BLUE

Am I blue
For you?
No longer.
I see
Something
Of you
In those
Brown eyes,
That almost
Curly hair,
That five-foot-five
Form,
In that self-
Sacrificing love
That is offered
To me.

N D Evans

THE SIMPLE TOUCH

A letter, phone call or just saying 'Hello',
can touch the heart of someone you know,
especially if they are feeling low,
but trying hard not to let it show.

This simple touch to show you care,
when in person you cannot be there,
can raise a smile and brighten the day,
of those fighting to keep despair away.

Sometimes in our busy lives we forget,
yet this can have such a comforting effect,
we lift the spirits of those in need,
and feel good for having done a good deed.

Julie Marie Laura Shearing

FOR THE FIRST TIME

Once upon a time,
Something happened to me,
It was the sweetest thing,
That ever could be,
It was a fantasy,
A dream come true,
It was the day I met you.

The first time you said I love you,
My heart sang its glory,
The stars played out a tune,
That's the first time I noticed your smile,
I smiled back and said, 'I love you too.'
You changed my world with just one smile,
And you took my heart with just one kiss.

Love is like magic,
And it always will be,
For love still remains,
Life's sweet mystery,
Love works in ways we don't understand.

What if I hadn't of noticed your smile?
Would we be here now?
It must be fate,
We must belong together,
Love at first sight you say,
I think love was just working its magic.

I've been waiting ages to see you,
I don't know why,
But there are three words I want to say,
These three words are close to my heart,
I hope you don't take them for granted,
And break them apart,
Here are the three words I was thinking of,
I love you,
I really do.

Laura Perkins

DEFEATED

Do I stay in this state?
Not feeling.
Do I go?
Leaving those I love behind.
Your arms are around me,
But I feel nothing.
What is hiding behind this veil of fog?
Do I really want to know?
Can I face the reality?
Can I be strong?
Every breath drawing me closer to the unknown,
Pulling me into its darkness.
The tear I shed is dry,
Draining my presence.
Dragged into the void,
Willing to follow.
Defeated by life,
Transparent to the world.

Kathryn Wilson

A TRUE FRIEND

As we should not judge a book by its cover
So we should not judge each other
A true friend is hard to find
But one who has an open mind
One who may not share your views
But whose friendship you will never lose
That is a real friend and there for you
So far between, so very few
Be there for them when they need a hand
To give, and love, and understand.

Joan Constantine

MY TOWN

Talk of the town
Everybody's down
Lift your head above the water
Know what it's like to drown
Teenagers with son and daughter
Breathe in the sugar beet fume
Seek what their future doesn't loom
The police too scared to name
Hide away out of this town in shame
They went wrong along the way
Government's the one to blame
The victims lose their say
Expense paid through our teeth
Why don't they listen to our call?
Council's riches beyond belief
No one's strong enough to stand up tall
This isn't my town, it is theirs
I've had enough of this dirt-lined street
Feel the knives in my back from the stares
Where else could we meet?
On the fields close by
When the summer flows
That's where my, our, future grows.

Richard Marshall-Lanes

MY FATHER

Father you were there for me when I was so small
You'd be there to pick me up whenever I would fall
You'd gently tend my grazes and kissed away my tears
Protect me with your big strong arms throughout my childhood years
And when it was Christmas time, you were still there for me
I'd hide and watch you place my presents underneath the tree
We didn't have much money but we'd have a day away
We'd eat ice cream together and we'd talk away the day
A father and a little child wrapped in each other's dreams
You told me so many stories and we'd talk about your schemes
To make a wooden bicycle and paint it midnight blue
I didn't want a metal one, just one made by you
I knew it would be magic and at night would fly away
You told me we'd fly round the moon until the light of day
Oh Dad though I'm now fully grown, I wish you were here right now
I know you were my stepdad, but I miss you Dad, and how.

Grace Divine

An Ode To Maria

How soft, how sweet you are,
God blesses souls like you,
Symbol of innocence, you are,
Your cheerfulness's vigour.

God'll pour on you bliss,
That you live without stress,
Look after health 'n' innocence,
You'll feel vigour in sense.

Whilst sins do hurt your heart,
Your sweet look sees age art,
Joy in heart offers love
Because it comes from above.

Mighty will set your light
And life will become bright,
And joy will become spring,
Life will joy to you bring.

Spirit of love feeds heart,
Like azure flowers in art,
You do have emerald eyes,
Your spirit never dies.

You are my guardian angel,
What miracle you spell,
To catch a falling star,
Wherever your thoughts are.

Where your heart does sing,
Do wear a pretty ring,
In this noble and strange world,
People love you, Marigold.

Milan Trubarac

PRAYER

Prayer is
My ongoing conversation
With You, Lord,
My moment to rest
Beneath the shadow of Your wing;
My chance
To be cleansed
Of any sin in my heart;
My embrace of the blessings
You are pouring into my life;
My opportunity
To uphold my loved ones to You;
And my place of refuge
In Your chamber,
In Your secret court
Where I offer up songs of worship
And hear You speak to me
In the middle of the day.
Gracious Father,
Teach me
To pray more.

Jennifer Anne F Messing

TOASTED BAGUETTE

French
A style to some
For the bedroom
Rushing from life
To friendship

Closeness was love
Poppies in fields

Sliced, pieces of life
Shake their hand
The crush of a shake
Never arrived

My teeth gleam
Milky Bar Kid

Bones do the walk
Shelve the talk
It be the right way
Cigs, butts in my face

Angels play the Christmas tune
No oasis of delight

Tinsel rushing the plank
Hell, I not be crushed
Tales not screws hold me down

18th the walk
Tigers gleam on nan bread

No way
Purple champagne
Sparkles live in baguettes
In a royal sort of way

Monkey's cackle
Peeling yellow thoughts

Mustard, Dijon
Grainy, tasty
Jean D'Arc
Toasted baguette

Anton Nicholas

SENSE OF FORGOTTEN

I sense a drowning behind the eye
Where memories lie in still sepia
It is you I seek

I sense a drowning behind the eye
Where thoughts dry the lips
And speech sits in sadness
It is you I seek

I sense a drowning behind the eye
Where tears lie dormant
And laughter's spilt in sour pools
It is you I seek

I sense a drowning here
Behind my eye -
Caught in a snapshot . . .
It is me I seek

Laura Wyer

I WONDER WEATHER

Oh vast infectious skies
Which overcast our eyes
You colour our moods
And distil our minds

Weathering thoughts
Which pass with the clouds
Cause me to wonder and scream aloud
Mute mentor
Who conducts the thunder?
Rules the wind and rain?
Reminding us mere mortals
We don't control the game

Putting life in perspective
My positive, my negative
Instilling calm
Threatening torment
A visual charm
An unpredictable element

You absolve me
You indulge me
You fascinate
Your light offers life
Your night is my fate

Rebecca Poole

LOVE WILL PASS

Your love will pass
Day will turn into night
I may pass, hard for you

It may hurt your heart
To see that your love has gone
To see how hard it is for you
Your love has to go away

Night will turn into day
And then they will always stay with you,
But night stars will pass

But it is soon over for you to see
Your love has come to pass.
The day has gone, night passes on
Your heart will see
It's gone out of your life.

Caitlin Kovacs (8)

JACK FROST

One mysterious night, I saw Jack Frost,
Scintillating, pirouetting in and out of my garden.
His skin was jagged and denticulated,
His eyes were crystal and ghostly
And he was so irregular.

As soon as he saw me, he leapt with caution,
All the way to the woods.
Finally I found that mystery figure.

Before he left, he nipped my fingers and toes.
Straight away he darted,
Leaving a sheet of magical powder.

Joel Smith (9)

SYNTHETIC FOOD

I liked our food when bread was rough
When gingernuts were really tough,
When cheese, it used to have a skin,
When meat was hung on a metal hook
And tasted good when it was cooked,
When milk in the bottle had cream on to,
When tomatoes used to have taste,
Now are an absolute disgrace,
Food didn't have a sell-by-date
And all of it tasted really great,
No plastic wrapping, it was fresh,
Even fish had tasty flesh,
Give me food that has no E's,
Give me food without disease,
Everything is so synthetic,
Could it be, it's all genetic?
Even sweets don't taste the same,
Health and hygiene are to blame,
We've gone mad on wrapping food,
Let's have some dirt, it might sound crude,
Let's have some food that tastes like food!

B Page

TONIGHT

Tonight,
I stepped upon a memory,
One I thought I'd lost along the way.
I was surrounded by people,
Singing, smiling,
No room for more.
But your spirit sat next to me.
I could feel your voice
Whisper in my ear,
I could feel your breath
In the song.
I heard you say
That you really loved me
Tonight.

Jerome Kiel

THE TRAVELLER'S DAUGHTER

I've been to so many different schools
That they're starting to look the same
No different are the sneering looks
When I'm forced to tell my name

Paint is peeling off the walls
The carpets wearing away
Damp patches on the ceiling
More boring day by day

Just some more names to remember
For faces I've all seen before
For them I'm just another new girl
Another kid to ignore

So I'll sit here quietly in the corner
I won't try to make a friend
What's the point? It's not long till
I pack my bags and leave again

Rehana Allison (14)

DESTINY

When I'm out I try to have a good time
I keep telling myself that all will be fine
But I'm bored and there's no way out
What is life all about?

I wish someone would tell me why I'm here
One day just whisper in my ear
Should I be a doctor, teacher or dancer?
It's got to the point where I need an answer

Is this all just testing me
Eventually leading mc to dcstiny?
Why can't someone just confirm?
Maybe it's something I have to learn

But what if it never gets to that
Then where will I be at?
Everything is so confusing
What options should I be choosing?

Everything's all up in the air
Life is complicated and unfair
How come some people just seem to know
Where in life they are supposed to go?

Andrea Crome

SUNSHINE THROUGH THE RAIN

My life has been eventful,
Not in the best of ways

I tried to see the sunshine,
Through all those rainy days

It never worked, hard as I tried
The sun had disappeared, left in its place, the rain

My life became bleak,
All I felt was anguish and pain

Maybe that's what drove me,
Drove me over the edge into a dark abyss

I couldn't see a way out,
All the good things I had, my mind would miss

That's when it happened,
Something I'll never forget

Not the best of choices, I must admit,
But something I'll never regret

It helped me to see,
To see the real me

Someone I hadn't seen in a while,
Someone my soul longed to be

I still hurt, always will
Still feel the anguish and pain

But now I feel happier
Because there is the sun, shining through the rain.

Sarah Jane Davies

LANCASHIRE COLLEGE

Lancashire College is the place to be,
Give it a visit, you'll like what you see.
The venue is pleasant, very well run,
Interesting courses can be quite fun.

Whatever your age, you will fit in,
Come, give it a go and let's begin.
The subjects vary from yoga to art,
All well-tutored, right from the heart.

Principal Helen is always about,
Any problems, she'll sort them out.
Facilities ace to fulfil your stay,
Polite, helpful staff in every way.

Some new interests will you stimulate,
Just enroll, don't leave it too late.
They cater for dieters and varied meals,
So very delicious, they always appeal.

Other students' company is good for you,
To share ideas, learn something new.
Once you find what it's all about,
You'll book again, no shadow of doubt.

Patricia Carter

UNHEARD COMMUNICATION

Love expands boundaries bordering on the Heaven above lust
Clouding the only sense of sensation
Care lost as your care is gained.

Life for that night is thriving
Our missed beat kills her
While she is trapped entwined in her own heart.

As the sun rises the world screams

My heart bursts
Hers opens as the bird flies her way
Unaware that his has been opened to another.

At sunset I communicate with love
Yet love never compromises.

Alice Rebecca Barton (16)

An Imaginary Painting

A woman sits in the lamp light
Her head bent over a china bowl,
Her eyes closed.
She's still half dreaming.

Her thick ginger hair has been down
Skirting all night, now strands fall
Over a face we'd call plain, but then
Men found that puffed paleness beautiful.

The lamp gives off an amber light
And the whiff of paraffin
She'll cover later with lavender oil.
Into cold water she'll waken,

And the hard pillow lines of sleep
Will lift out of her pinking cheek.
Or so I imagine it might have been
When women washed in bowls at dawn,

And lamplight smelled. Face creams
Have not been invented yet,
But she has inherited tricks for beauty
Like handstands for shining eyes

Pinching for rosiness
Biting for plump red lips
Smiling for lines going kind ways
And singing for a lilt in speech.

As looking glasses are rare and tainted
This woman belongs to herself.
She feels good in her skin
At home in her beauty. Whole within.

Janis Mackay

A Soul To Bare

Is the soul like a precious flower, just waiting to be discovered;
each petal an expression of life?
Each step closer bringing feelings of being mothered;
each step back from trouble and strife.

As each petal falls what new beauty, what new experience will
we find revealed?
As each new moment passes the clock, what new secrets lie
beneath, concealed?

When we seek an increase in our spiritual awakening, a place to begin;
we have the tools of prayer and meditation, the means to find the
answers within.

With faith and much patience, with years of much testing; the whys
and the wherefores are replaced by new visions of -
ah, now how interesting.

In essence if we can see each new experience as an opportunity for
growth, there is no real reason for fear, no real need for sloth.

As the soul is made bare, it's like finding yourself with old lovers;
there is something familiar, something wonderful within ourselves
and others.

When we let go of old patterns we awaken the new, not always the
expected, not always the same view.

A new realization may dawn, that things only happen as they are
meant to. No need to force anything; for the coming of the season
gives us that clue.

In time the soul is glimpsed, as though some great torch has been shone.
Here there is no place for fear; like nudity a different kind of light is
switched on.

Beyond all the obscurations can be found rapture, beauty, everlasting
love. We can be graced with the tranquillity of the peaceful dove.

With time a new dawning may pass, that the journey inward is a journey outward, and that we've come full circle - at last.

There is no more them and us, no more I or she. What I do to others is what I do to me.

There is no more this world and that world, no more taunts of perverse. For we are the very breath from our bodies; the very stars of our universe.

We come to learn that the spirit is love . . . so, so many things.

David Barnett

CHEERS

To wear pretty things next to the skin
Makes one feel good,
To walk in the sunshine
To breathe the fresh air,
It's good to be alive.
To listen to the news more than once a day
Becomes tedious to say the least.
Depression could easily set in,
It's best to look around,
Better things can be found
To cheer a dismal day.

P Wright

Evening Charm

Sitting on the edge of town
Relaxing in the new era or the old one
Thinking of the cause yet never won
Weeping in time for his loved one
Seeming to express once again
Oh that's right was there once
She had noticed the cherry tree
In the shades of new times then
Those early days in strife had to come
Colonies, states, soldiers, servants, yes
Long ago pavements knew different days.

Malachy Trainor

AVALON HERE

Avalon - art thou the ephemeral home of my soul?

Art thou oh harbour of my heart's full chalice?

Within thy dew-laden swirling mists surround
Ghostly grey horse-mounted knights abound
Comforting, protecting, could I be a seeker found

Avalon - yea Avalon rising upon yonder peak I spy
Floating on clouds ringed rainbow high
Silent now as a breeze flown sigh

Oh Avalon - remember my age toilsome journey then
Through ravaging times and pitiless spent
Wrought of heart and cascading tears did vent

The beaten dirt road that leads to your gate
Towards love and joy fast away from the world of hate
There to sit in quiet solitude my pondering life's fate

Yea Avalon, within thy walls oh safe haven bidden
Enemy and foe both shrouded then hidden
To be buried 'neath green turves thence called their midden

Avalon, oh Avalon, give succour to this soul who finds you now
Harbour me under your leafy canopy and bough
Inside thy stout protective walls of granite to me thy vow

Here, at last I can breathe this my breath of comfort to know
These my selves of spectral beings bright with light
do merge now whole
To form this my diversity of mind, body, spirit and soul

Avalon, oh Avalon, of seemingly mythical epic story told
I know now your existence is real through ages old
Be then my life's sanctuary as my time upon this plane here unfolds

Oh reader shush - quiet now thou of your mind and soul
Look to thine own life journey and see thy whole
Complexity of simpleness yes - but oh so wondrous to behold

M Boase

UNTITLED

The unhappiness is
like a wave
hanging from my intellect
over my face and down
into my heart.
That I must fight on
pulls at me
yet I know as numbing
as all this is
I can go on
and will find an
end to this
in the consolation of my soul
unto joy and peace -
of character laid down the line
and a cleared and washed deck.

Paul Barron

FOR ONE TURNING TWENTY-ONE

Now that you are twenty-one,
the game of life, yet not even half won.
Its struggles haven't yet begun.
Its mysteries yet to be undone.

Neither is life a sweet dream,
that you wake up to and smile.
Nor is it a nightmare
that bothers you all the while.

Life is not gauged by the pounds you lose,
or the dollars you earn.
It might not always go the way you choose,
and you might have to take a turn.

Neither is life's worth just a penny,
Nor is time's worth just a dime.
May your deeds be lauded by many,
making yours a worthwhile lifetime.

May your life be filled with love,
compassion and the will to give.
You are twenty-one now.
A long way to go before you take a bow.

Prasad Rajendran

I'M CONCERNED

I'm concerned about nuclear missiles for they endanger the
                                                    safety of Earth
For it's humanity's place of birth,
I'm concerned about racism and the brutality against a race
Or the way the rainforests are cut down at an alarming pace,
And I'm concerned about any economic depression
Plus I hate it when people are kept under repression.
I'll tell you a confession,
Of all these things man hasn't yet learnt his lesson,
Yes, I'm bothered about the pollution of the air, land and sea
And the increasing of cars on roads for people like you and me,
And I'm distressed about Man's downward trend
For once good morals he used to depend,
Yes, I'm troubled about the cruelty and killing of animals
Since they're an asset to man and should be valuable,
And I'm worried about the escalating of crime
For we're living in such bad times.
Or what about the starving millions or the poor
And all the people that are killed in wars?
For most of the time when there's a problem man is the cause
Such as starting wars and the breaking of laws,
I'm very concerned as you can see, about things that affect
                                                    you and me.

Donato Genchi

CHOICES

A child has run from within us
When are we grown, when are we free
Or captive, when life takes form
We know we cannot be
No more dances in the rain
No more simple parts to play
To look at what life's offering means
Simplicity has left again
Broken, reborn this protective shell which set us loose to see
What to make of this parcel of uncertainty
Which follows like fog stalking ships at sea

Bryony Freeman

IN THE PERMANENT SUN

Complications are few in the sun
We stay young forever
Safe in the permanent sun
Coming a year troubles no more

We drink to the sun
No more in the shade
Young in the permanent sun
A new year with no care

Walking as free as the air
Eternal happiness lighting the way
See the path stretching before you
Wide as the sands of time

The world's at your feet
Relaxing in the permanent sun.

Carole A Cleverdon

WARNING TO ALL

On Monday I was feeling ill
Nausea and headaches, so I took a pill
But the feeling just wouldn't shift
So I went to bed to try and cope with it

My eldest son was just as bad
His stomach hurt and he felt sad
So we both took to our beds
Tried to sleep to clear our heads

By Tuesday we were joined by hubby
And youngest son was feeling yucky
We shut the doors, turned up the heat
Was it the 'flu making us so weak?

Drowsy Wednesday, still in bed
Stabbing pains piercing through my head
Early afternoon, I heard an alarm
Reactions were instant - keep my children from harm

Off with the boiler, open the doors
Called out the gasman to find the cause
Evacuated the house and went outside
When there's gas in the house there is nowhere to hide

The carbon monoxide detector had sounded
Concerns for our health were proved to be founded
The CO gas has no smell and is clear
Without the alarm we'd be dead I fear

It's only six months since my boiler was serviced
The CO leakage back then did not surface
So I'm telling you all, please buy an alarm
It may be the one thing keeping your family from harm

Karen Giles

AS ONE

When darkness falls and night draws in
And silence fills my sleeping home
I lie awake and wait for sleep
And for the dreams that never come.

Then as I drift off suddenly
I'm wakened by the woeful sound
Of fear and cries of evil dreams
That look for you until you're found.

I cannot understand your cries
Or stop the dreams from finding you
But maybe I can stop the things
That are making you feel tired and blue.

Does anyone know just how it feels
To hear your child so full of pain?
A pain that's caused by other's ills
By hateful words said o'er again.

I cannot bear to listen more
To endless cries of fear and hate
And so tomorrow I will go
To meet you by the old school gate.

And I will stop the chants and hits
That make your life a lengthy fight.
And I will keep you safe at home
From early morn 'til late at night.

No more will others cause you pain.
Nor will you suffer at their hands.
For I'll protect you from now on
And now as one, we both will stand.

Karen Smith

WEALTH!

Awaken from the sleep!
Burning sun . . .
creeps the window . . . thrusting my lazy eyes.
Greeneries shake
to the rhythm of the beat
dancing flawlessly . . . pitching the breeze.
Birds in the air
chirping blissfully . . . to unknown destiny.
I said my prayer,
hurriedly . . . squirming on the couch.
Oh! my Creator,
granting me . . . breath
the purest wealth . . . I want.
I saw your smile
merrily . . . slumbering on the bed.
Oh! my Creator
blessing me . . . a beautiful companion
the joy of my heart
longing one . . . I crave for.
A new lease of life . . .
certainly,
for today . . . and every day
till the end of . . .
time.

Raffi Sharwan

CHILDPROOF FORMAT

With each aspiring headache
It gets more difficult
To give up the bottle
And contemplate surrendering
To a blister pack.

A Lee Firth

PAIRS

Sausage and mash
Steak and kidney
Fish and chips
Smoke and chimney
Night and day
Bacon and eggs
Bucket and spade
Lazy and heads
Bread and butter
Sugar and spice
Salt and pepper
Once or twice
Cheese and biscuits
Chicken and pox
Pins and needles
Jack and the box
But the best pair of all
Is husband and wife,
Not the slang term
Of trouble and strife!
God planned love and marriage
When two hearts combine,
To face ups and downs:
He turned water into wine
At that wedding when Jesus
Rejoiced as He blessed
God's plan for mankind -
Marriage vows happiness.

Marion Skelton

COLOUR PALETTE

The sunset bleeds on Crimson Lake
With cloud shadows of burnt umber.
How I feared my heart would break
Ere I to eternal slumber,

With cloud shadows of burnt umber,
You are the palest Chinese white,
Ere I to eternal slumber
Consummation's height.

You are the palest Chinese white
Your tousled hair glows Titian red,
Consummation's height
Tangled limbs and rumpled bed.

Your tousled hair glows Titian red
The glass contrasts in Prussian blue,
Tangled limbs and rumpled bed
Bitter poison's a darker hue.

The glass contrasts in Prussian blue
How I feared my heart would break,
Bitter poison's a darker hue
The sunset bleeds in Crimson Lake.

C M Welch

TSUNAMI

Unstoppable disaster.
Water burying all
Whirling waves of devastation.
No respect for saving souls.
Bodies unrecognisable, swollen, turgid and unclaimed.
Memories living for ever in reluctant survivors
Relieved yet guilty for their escape.
Material assets no longer important.
Lost lives left behind
Thousands never found
Cruel nature.
Tsunami.

Gael Nash

Zoo

On this side of life
Death is not proud.
Free from the chains
Of morality,
Nature igneous machines
Sword beak, poisonous glands,
Swift foot, sharp teeth,
Wiry tongue, iron claw,
Sturdy sinew, slippery body,
Changing colour, stony bark,
Feathered foot, keen sight,
All united by the singular
Purpose to survive.

J Emmanuel

ENOUGH IS ENOUGH

I don't want to explain
Please, don't make me
Increase your pain
Just keep in mind
I'm the only one to blame
And please, go away
I wanna be alone now
I wanna go on
On my own
Maybe I am selfish
But I think it's far time
To get back my life
It's not that I don't like it that way
But I think it's time to change it again
I just believe
Life is too short
To be lived
The same way
Day after day.

Tatiana Bonatti Peres

ANOTHER ME

Look deep into these tired crying eyes, can you see another me?
Hiding away from the risk of hurt, alone I fill my days.
My soul has been shattered, the faith I have no more,
If I break away you cannot see or know the real person who is me.
Sometimes I break down and cry, this fight I feel gets too much.
The everyday struggle, the forever upward hill, a break I do not
                                                    seem to make.

This time has never touched me, no happiness has my heart ever felt.

Z Fitzjohn

ASIAN BAKE

It came from the depths
Sweeping aside luxurious filth,
But in the process
Many innocents were killed,
With dollar bills
They grilled in the baking sun,
Baking, post quaking disaster,
With the aqua as the carrier
Your lackey, your mule,
To give out cholera and dysentery,
In a most affable manner
That cares not a jot
For status or stature,
Pray for Mother Nature's mercy.

C T W P Darkly

A Girl Named Sue

Her name is Sue Young, she's a hero unsung
So please do not worry when she's in a hurry
A tad hyperactive but truly proactive
With a good deal of nerve and a steep learning curve

Who lives for the minute, she's in it to win it
If she had to slow down she would probably drown
A geography queen with direction supreme
She is simply the best, north, south, east and west

Complete with true zest not one minute to rest
If she gets in a flap she refers to the map
It's devotion with motion without action subtraction
She can aim at a star, it won't be too far

Better to burn out and follow your dream
Than rust out through thinking and to never have been
So here's to a hero and all credit is due
To an all round professional who we all know as Sue.

E Simcock

NEW BEGINNINGS FOR US ALL

As we sit and sip champagne what is there for us to gain?
Another year begins for everyone of us
But do we all know what this world has laid out for us to unfold?

Aren't we glad we will never know 'cause if that was the case
We would wish for all the sadness to never be aglow
Or even show.

So please take one day at a time
And tell your loved ones how much you care
Even if you are never there.

As we make our resolutions don't we often wish we had the
Right solution to life and taking everything in our stride
With so much pride with our little angels at our sides.

They say angels are up above through God's love
Don't ever think 'cause they're now in Heaven above
You have lost their love.

Just talk to them each new day of this year
And you will hear them softly whispering in your ear.
Don't be afraid to cry on this New Year's Day 'cause it's just
Your angels being with you in their own special way.

Anastasia Williams Cowper

RHAPSODY AT THE SUNDAY MORNING SUPERMARKET GARAGE

Viewing from a double-decker bus
I can see all the many cars
Crowding the reeking pumps; hungry for petrol.

Christmas now behind us, the hunger
Grows greater, that need for fuel;
Consumption of the world, the way we've always been.

Those many cars in muted colours
All looking similar: how is that done?
Neither by you nor me, but by generations, unthinking;

Waging wars in the long past;
The close past; the fallout's distinct.
Our leader won't get away

With another grin on TV
Placating us, uneasy revellers
of Planet Civilisation

In which the rules are in place,
As if to ask, 'Where's any other choice?'

God knows, we need a new beginning.

Mike Green

To Hail a Brand New Year

What's all this fuss and bother
About another brand new year
When for many folk around us
The prospect only brings more fear
More tanks, more bombs, more guns
More daily pictures confronting us
Of weeping adults and limbless little ones
How do we have the nerve
To be happy and to cheer
When half the world is crying
Not wanting to face another new year
There's no money that can put things right
Only the will of man
So all of you with the urge to fight
Lay down your arms if you can
And in the peaceful moment following
The whole world can cheer
And everyone, yes everyone
Can hail a brand new year.

Daphne Fryer

THE COMPOST BIN

Fertilise me,
Light, soft, fluffy, brown, cloud-like.
Fill me,
Flowers too and nightingales perfected in death.
More, more, more.
As it enters, it strokes the core of my core.
Sweet pleasure to monitor your progress,
Every so often,
To stop and pat you down,
Thicken and solidify your minerals with
The spade of superciliousness.
Then . . .
Parasites; the leach, the roach.
Breeding, multiplying,
Questioning teeth, feet, antennae claw
Like tiny sharp hooks.
The wound of monstrous light appears gawping
In the beautiful self-consuming darkness.
I am ruined.
As the horse manure and weeds fall from me,
I cannot help but square an already fatal situation.
Multiply myself by myself with the rake of insecurity.
Even that is failed maths.
Suicide.

Naila Machob

WHAT IS OUR LIFE?

Every act through life is like a word
That floats on the wind like a bird.
It's there in all we think or speak
Like a twig the bird held in its beak.
Every action the worst or best
Is there to build up our life's nest.

Every part of life is just a wish
That floats along like a tiny fish.
From normal minds somehow we hide
Like a fish on another new tide.
Through good or bad our life we trail
Each dream did grow like a fish's tail.

Each part of life we have to learn
That slides each day like a worm.
Every note that comes from every sound
Like a serpent feeding off the ground.
Through right or wrong each one a goal
Like that worm we poke through that hole.

Each act of our life's a simple vowel
That ends up wise like a barn owl.
Like a tree or bush coming into fruit
Most of us don't notice or give a hoot.
Then light or darkness we slowly eye
Like all the creatures we live, we die.

Colin Allsop

SAFE-WAY MEAT

I like meat that's neat in a good square meal.
No gristle, no bone,
No flavour of its once-farmed freedom.

My steaks should be well done,
No blood or hint of this muscle's previous work.
I do not want to be reminded after a day at the office
Of the life I now eat,
The breath stopped by a bolt gun that I now bolt down
To keep myself breathing.

The cellophane forest
Is my hunting ground
Where I stalk with moral ambiguity
The next meal of my day.

I feel no affinity with the bringer of this feast.
The carer of lamb and calf
Who sits cold in February's embrace
Watching as the steam and blood
And pain of life's first breath
Condenses innocently on a newborn's first mother call.

Nor even, when a wilder food graces the menu,
With the tenant of the cold morning and gun
Who with four-legged friend
And barrel breach armed breaches the gap,
Between life and death and food.

Bring me steak, bring me stew,
Bring me pan-fried partridge, jugged hare, warm pigeon salad,
A slow-roasted-oven-basted-free-range-feast.
But without the responsibility
For that is too distant from my plate
And I have washed my hands of my appetite's salvation.

David Gatward

TIME OUT

Where would I be but here at ease,
Away from the hustle, hue and cry:
Just me . . . in a symphony of rustling leaves,
Sibilance of turquoise seas,
Distant sounds flung off the breeze:
Where raising of a dreamy eye
Is lost within an infinite sky
And thoughts are only there to tease
And flutter with the butterfly.

Colleen Biggins

SAY CHEESE!

There is Gruyère, and there's Feta:
One's from Switzerland, one Greece.
In whichever land they come from,
Each is known as 'The Big Cheese'!

That's what my good friend told me;
This friend of mine's called Bob.
His favourite's Gorgonzola,
Which he calls 'The Italian Job'!

My friend is a comedian
Who does not like French cheese much;
But he loves Edam and Gouda,
And he calls them 'Double Dutch'!

For all you fans of British cheese,
I have good news to bring:
Of all the cheeses in the world
A poll says Cheddar's king!

Roger Williams

'MIDST THE CONFRONTATIONS

When the tornado of ruinous fate
Draws close to the chambers of heart
Neither a spark or hope looms to rescue
Nor a balm to provide relief from agony
'Midst the confrontations.

Aloof from the prospects of all hopes
Dragged afar from the corridors of joy
I feel cornered by the die-hard doom
With ravaging undercurrents of gloom
'Midst the confrontations.

The bright dawn surrenders to sunset
The beautiful flowers wilt hastily, upset
O! Every beginning has an ordained end
But, can every curve face an abrupt end
'Midst the confrontations.

Thorns on one path, petals on another
In hope's search I tread both together
But the abrupt paths now stand in front
Ditched and wrecked, how can I confront
'Midst the confrontations.

T Ashok Chakravarthy

GRATITUDE TO MY MOM

To my mama so precious and rare
With the passage of time treats me with love and care
And asks for nothing in return, not even a dime
Joys and sorrows together sublime.

When troubles surround me and I am tired and distressed
There she stands by my side, helps me face the rest
Helping me through all my trials and tribulations
Only with love, care, patience and affection.

And if I ever had a chance to wish
I'd wish for getting Mama's nature so precious and rich
Blessed and nourished with all the goodness that life can share,
That's my mama, so precious and rare.

Shalini Menezes

APPARITION

Lost soul left behind,
In the shadows of a room.
His voice speaks through your mind
Whispering through and through.
Feel the presence of the ghost
Touch the windows filled with frost
Communicate with the ones you love the most
At no matter what cost
Crack a joke if you must
Because of your discomfort
You distrust
But the apparition
Wasn't from your imagination
It was from your heart, where you cried
Where no one can say you lied.

Conor McGreevy

A Dream Of A Magic Carpet

Picture this, picture me,
Sixty seconds till sixty minutes
Movements in shadows,
Visions in lights,
Happiness in a circle,
Loneliness lost in a box.

As a boy I dreamed of a magic carpet,
Exciting, inviting,
A make-believe world within youth.

Cold days, cold nights,
Frozen hands, lost gloves,
Cuts on fingers, pain to feel,
A moment that's real when you're
Eight years old.

A dream of the magic carpet
Wasn't going to leave me.
Young and a silly billy,
What else matters but tea and jelly,
Wacky Races on the telly,
Colourful, wonderful,
A dream of a magic carpet.

Andrew Ryan

TALKING

My mother never stopped talking.

As a teacher she talked all day to the children, telling them,
'Come here,' 'Go there,' 'Behave yourself, what do you think
you're doing?'
in that special pitched voice that they must be taught at college -
along with arithmetic for five-year-olds, reading for six-year-olds,
geography for seven-year-olds, RE for everyone -
that voice that reaches to the back of the classroom and beyond,
then when she came home, she told us all about her day,
how dim the children were, how hard it was to get them to listen
and 'What on Earth are they going to do with their lives if
they can't add two and two together and get a respectable answer?'
and, 'What have you been doing at school today?'
and, 'Did you remember to take your plimsolls?'
and her voice rolled on never waiting for an answer.

And the years went on and I heard my mother's voice
talking on the telephone to one of her school cronies,
I heard her berating the paper boy for being late with her newspaper -
sometimes I heard her murmuring quietly to one of the grandchildren
when she thought no one was about -
I heard her telling the politicians on television what she thought
of their feebleness, joining in 'Question Time' with great gusto,
or cheering Arsenal on in the Cup Final.

In the fifty years I knew her she never seemed to stop talking.
So I didn't have a chance to tell her anything,
I thought she never heard *my* cries, *my* dreams, *my* prayers,
until at the end, before that last painful breath,
she smiled at me and said,
'We've been alright, haven't we?'

Ann Rust

DRUGGED

The opiate of the masses;
administered every day,
is *sport,* in all its many forms;
those various games we play.

Nothing wrong - for youngsters,
amateurs and the like;
but then used by British governments,
to drug 'us' day and night.

Why, this need to stupefy,
dim our wits, our brains;
what do successive governments -
our country, really stand to gain?

'Stupidity' is the answer,
have no doubts at all,
for it keeps the vast majority,
'enclosed' within high walls.

'Control' is yet the other side,
of this devious political game,
we are easier to 'manipulate'
and that's their crafty aim!

'They' don't want 'intelligence',
people who can think;
might ask awkward questions,
kick up all sort of stinks!

'Indoctrinate' our women
with a selection of TV soaps,
with sport for all and sundry,
but - especially British blokes!

Peter Mahoney

A Day In Romantic Paris

In the Paris elegant air,
The young cheeks of the lovers are there.
Strolling along the River Seine to and fro,
With their hearts all aglow.
They drift into the perfume shops,
Scented sweet as a variety of flowers,
Some escape the gathering of busy crowds
By going up the mighty Eiffel Tower
To dine on the terraces
As the accordion band races
With the tune of can-can!
Whilst the lilac dresses of the ladies go up and down,
Almost the speed of a merry-go-round.
As they look down below,
The Arch De Thrispe seems to flow
Up towards Champs Elysée
And seeing the famous arch is a seething reward
Before loving couples homeward affairs
And tomorrow is once again theirs.

Sammy Michael Davis

ABANDONED

Recently, while enjoying late tea within the confines of my lorry, towards me limped a pathetic, bedraggled, rib thin, mongrel dog. It was glaringly obvious he was about to beg.

Offering a sandwich, my heart went out to the poor beast, every minute crumb was devoured at what I would call . . . choking speed.

Calculating his mistrust of the human species, he wandered into the night. Who could blame him?

It's beyond comprehension why some people disregard their responsibilities, in this case to an animal more than likely to be an affectionate, loyal companion.

On each occasion when visiting this particular part of the country, my eyes scanned the area . . . to no avail.

Hopefully, he is now a member of a family . . . a family who will give him all anybody ever needs in life . . . love and affection.

Who would fail tae bow their heid
The height according to your need
But not for any lavish feed
To stave off hunger . . .
On second thought, a crust or two you would exceed
With rancorous plunder.

Was it him who condemned you to beg for crisis
Left you to your own devices
With a stomach on its knees, and twice as wanting,
All reflected in your eyes . . .. the dice as daunting.

Poor beast! A victim o' a material standing
A victim o' intense commanding
A victim, his, he would always abandon
To suit his style,
For him . . . the Lord Almighty will be the hangman's stand-in
With yon halter, vile!

David Russell McLean

A SMILE

Smiling is infectious,
If you smile and pass it on
One small smile can then become
The beginning of a lot of fun.

Did you smile a smile today
As you went along the way?
And did the people smile at you,
Or was it just the normal few?

It doesn't cost you money,
But just for a short while,
It could make you very rich,
If you give away a smile.

Doreen E Hampshire

HEART OF KIND

What of this unearthly thing
New heaven on Earth shy quiet
Why well his face and tortured mind
Tears shining in his searching eyes
Heart of kind and tenderness full
This unearthly thing
This thing called love
What now my frantic prayer to comfort you don't try
This restless man what of your soul
Edge of Hell walking
Pale soft face in splendour of the moon
Lost as a troubled child in an empty room
Heart of kind and tenderness full
This unearthly thing
This thing called love

Beryl Barlow

ADDICTION LAND

Addiction Land has you by the hand,
Come dance, dance, dance in Addiction Land

Addiction Land is affliction land,
And you will do as we command, in Addiction Land

Addiction Land is poison land
And you might know, but understand,
You've no control in Addiction Land.

Addiction Land must make a stand
A moo cow's brand to show who owns in Addiction Land

Addiction Land is a fiction land,
But in your head, if hope is dead,
Your myths are fed in Addiction Land

Addiction Land is boomtown land
We make 'em merry 'afore they gag'
And wish they'd never smoked the fag
And bought into Addiction Land

Addiction Land supplies demand,
Each new career so carefully planned, to see you cold - a lifeless fan
The only way out of Addiction Land

Addiction Land will treat you grand
Keep you poor - when you're no more, watch you lowered to the floor
Can you see us cry? As that sludgy sand
Covers your coffin from Addiction Land.

Raymond Barber

TRANSCENDENT MIND

The impossible dream come true, to live in perfect peace
as the mind is transcendent from its earthly trauma,
and has overcome fear and anxiety. As the mind's eye views
this dismal world from above the clouds, so shining and quiet.
Never a sound nor any whimper, no sense of
fear or delusion, only quiet and content felt in the heart.
I have departed from the hell-bent pace of the madding
crowds and travelled to a state of mind far away high
above it all. No trauma exists here, and no trouble,
only tranquil blissful peace and shining beauty.
Only angels exist here, there is no evil, no sound of word
that offends, only quiet peace and the whispers from
God's mouth, whispers of peace, love, joy and truth.
There is no body or earthly form, only heavenly light,
I love this heavenly bliss here, never shall I leave this
place in my mind so high above the clouds.
Forever I will remain as one with this blissful shining,
beautiful place, never to return to the trauma and misery
of earthly living, so full of trouble, strife and misgiving.
Here I am and here I must stay as one with absolute
peace, no evil to mar my joy forever and ever.

Antony Lees

EASTER TIDE

The beach was a vast expanse today,
The tide was out a long, long way,
The waves did roll as they chewed up the sand,
The sight was beautiful, rather quite grand!
Little ponds were left as moats around the rocks,
Kiddies were playing without shoes and socks,
Dogs were swimming in the sea by the caves,
A few bodies braved the cold as they rode the waves,
The air was cool, but the sky was bright
Easter tide, a sheer delight.

Theresa Hartley

TO LIVE OR DIE

The old die young; the young die old
Or at least so I'm told
I dare not experience either way
For I just want to live today.
But if anger is red and envy is green,
Then does jealousy lie in-between?
It's a dying nation outside that door
Something I've seen more than once before
Where no one knows if they should come or go -
Am I alive or dead? - I just don't know
It's legal to kill when you're at war
But boy oh boy, it was not like that before
Where you could be damned for one mistake
In this world that is so fake
For you risk freedom, just being awake.

Graham Connor

A NEW BELIEVER

I wasn't one, but then I saw the light
Shining down upon you what a beautiful sight.
Hands so tiny, hard to grasp
Small little legs up to one's a***
A shadow of hair on the top of your face
You lie there and wriggle with so much grace.
To think that once you were just an egg,
Dividing each day to make arms and legs.
Isn't it wonderful how a life so small
Could grow up big and so tall.
With a mind of your own no one can guess,
The future ahead of you, *what is best?*
The world is such a very big place
Lots to explore trimmed with lace
Awareness now, there are things that don't seem right,
Listen to your heart, it will tell you your plight.
But remember always He can help you
To guide you, fill you with love in all that you do.
He is only a whisper or thought away,
He doesn't mind what you say.
He will listen as He did to me
God is everywhere. He is free.

Jan Nice

What's For Tea Tonight Mum?

'What's for tea tonight Mum?
Oh no, not fish, it's yuk!
It's scaly and it's slimy
And the bones in your throat get stuck!

I hate the way those eyes stare back
As it sits upon my plate,
And my stomach turns at the memory
Of the maggots involved in its fate.

My granny likes fish to be boiled,
Cos it's soft and kind to her gums,
My mum says fish is good for me,
But whoever took notice of mums?

Now I don't mind fish from the chippie,
All hot and wrapped in a bag,
And I'll even swallow a cockle or two,
But the thought of raw fish makes me gag!

With so many fish to choose from,
Why would anyone want to eat squid?
Its rubbery legs are all chewy,
And that's not good news for a kid.

Now I didn't know fish could have fingers,
And fish in a cake sounds all wrong,
But hey, fish now comes in a burger,
So I might just let that near my tongue.

I couldn't be one of those fishermen,
Going out in my boat before dawn,
Just waiting around for those fish to bite,
Would surely make me yawn.

I've nothing against those creatures,
Who spend all their days in the sea,
But I'd much rather see them swimming,
Than joining some chips for my tea!'

Shaunagh Cole

GRAVITY

You've restricted me,
Pulled me to you,
Captured and held me,
Introduced and kept me for yourself
For an eternity.

I'm stuck here. Trapped. Bounded by your force
You leave me here, alone whilst
You are silent,
Wandering the Earth like a
Lonely stranger
Laughing silently behind closed doors.

I want to be free
From your ways of attraction,
You've cast a spell
And shattered my freedom.

I can't leave, but I don't want to stay,
Your force encircles me,
Enchants me,
And calls me to you.

My breath is panting,
I'm exhausted by your will,
My attempts to jump high,
And soar have failed,
My power is no match for yours,
I fall. I surrender.

Selina Mirpuri

THREE BLIND PIGS

Three blind pigs, three blind pigs;
See how they eat, see how they eat.
They all got drunk on the swill they did,
Then ran off without paying the bill, they hid,
Did you ever see such a pink thrill, to kid,
As three blind pigs, three blind pigs;
See how they drink, see how they drink,
Pissed as a parrot, ran after a milkman's float
Got crushed by a crate of the gold top coat
It smashed on the floor and did cream them alive
And made for my desk, some pure raw skive
Three blind pigs, three blind pigs . . .

Anthony Rosato

THE JOURNEY

Feeling quite strange as though lost in a dream
My gaze was transfixed down below at the scene

A girl so familiar was asking the way
An old man was pointing when I heard him say

'There is only one route from here you can take
Just follow the road till you come to the lake

At which point you'll see the road split into two
The right road to take must be chosen by you.'

The girl started walking not really sure why
Unable to help, I could only stand by

The unending road seemed to stretch out for miles
Her feet sore and blistered, she stopped for a while

Then like a mirage in the distance ahead
The edge of the lake as the old man had said

Came into her view it wouldn't be long
She must keep on going, she had to be strong

Nearing the end of her journey at last
Facing two roads, there were scenes from her past

Which road to take only she could decide
A beckoning light seemed to draw her inside

But as she stepped forward we both heard a name
I realised that we were both one and the same

I knew I must reach her and make myself seen
From somewhere inside me I started to scream

The roads were both pathways to live or to die
The girl was my soul now, I understood why

Together as one we went back to the lake
Still hearing our name we knew which road to take

I opened my eyes hearing voices that said,
'She's out of the coma, thank God she's not dead.'

Helen King

NIGHT CALL

Someone told me a dream last night
She was all round and warm
As if stung by a whole swarm
She was middle-aged
Middle of what age I asked?
She was all round and warm
Inviting . . . lovely too.

She was a reflection
A happening
Oh that I saw a ritual
And more besides
That time would still
Awakening spawn - homage to the dawn
At full heat born of satisfaction
Give me a map to find my way
And I will as a whisper in a reflection
Or fire out of the morning mist
Charged by passion - heat
Entering bones

Drying the mouth
Still as the tongue of fire rests
No more night prayer to sacrifice
Fire bitten particles hurled skyward
Earthquake of belly molten grit
Yet more flames dying
And forked flame split

Fire, the mother of heat
Hungry, devoured the flame sheet
Or stuck by the thin flame fork
Walls and columns raised and fallen
Yet the same consume
And spit forth blank purity.

Spirit fire, I call on thee
Bend not burning bush nor tree
For some old flame
Will burn eternally
And in that flame
I will see my perfect vision of thee.

Clive Cornwall

ASHDOWN FOREST

Old Ashdown Forest is a place
For bishops to be called 'Your Grace'
For dogs to run, and planes to fly,
An everlasting mystery
Old Ashdown Forest, by and by
A grassy space beneath the sky
On sunny days with bright blue sky
An everlasting mystery
Come, sun and shower awaits us now
After the winter's hail and snow
On sunny days with bright blue sky
An everlasting mystery.

Peter Buss

TWISTED FATE

Strong feelings hidden inside,
Anger, passion, will they collide?
My mind filled to the brim,
Lost thoughts no longer swim.

Can it be what it ought to be?
Have I found what will set me free?
Withered dying emotions,
Washed away by drowning oceans.

Heated fury does not hide.
Power overcomes stride by stride.
Distant lonely dreams,
Haunted by helpless screams.

Come take what has been reaped.
Never knowing how far I leaped.
Visions ruled by my glory,
Twisted fate in this endless story.

Evelyne Germaine Vanderlinden

SHORT AND SWEET

I wish I were your duvet
to keep you warm at night
I would wrap myself around you
and hug you with all my might
and as the night grew colder
I would squeeze you even more
but just enough to keep you warm
so I wasn't thrown upon the floor.

Nikki Jackson

WONDERFUL STROLL

The sun's final ray
    Has left its sweet ember
Trees fold their branches
    As nightfall descends,
The badger has babies
    She needs to be tender
And birds chatter secrets
    To all of their friends.
I'm left alone, it used to warn danger
    But something has happened
        To the songs that I sing,
My being is drenched
    In magnificent splendour
By the rays of the master
    Who wills me to win.
So I hoot with the owls
    I fear darkness no longer
I'm more than a lifetime
    Away from control,
The circles I form
    Are joined to the wonder
And the path that I've taken
    Is a wonderful stroll.

Andrew Hobbs

HOME IS WHERE YOUR HEART IS

(Sunshine on the mountain)

Home is a place where your heart is,
And with your smile the sun now shines,
It's taken a long time to find out,
It's love that counts each time.

I see the kids playing in the backyard,
And Mom with washing on the line,
It's been a long time since I've been here,
And seen your face, well that's just fine.

I thought that this world was my oyster,
A life of freedom was so great,
A big mistake to think that's everything,
And realise 'fore it's too late.

You rent apartments by the dozen,
Careers and fun without any cares,
But what have you got when you return there?
A lonely room with empty chairs.

Home is a place where your heart is,
And with your smile the sun now shines,
It's taken a long time to find out,
It's love that counts each time.

Jonathan Grave

POPE JOHN PAUL II

The Catholic warrior prince,
A champion Pope of reconciliation,
Having lived through fear and intimidation,
In many foreign lands he has reached out with hope,
From the holy Vatican, St Peter's Square in Rome,
He has pledged his life to God of Heaven,
He the greatest Pope of all,
Of heavenly principals,
A miracle worker for his people,
Where justice and righteousness,
Go hand in hand,
For the downtrodden, the poor and the weak,
His voice has echoed around the world,
With a message of love, peace and unity,
To all the countries that still preach war,
He has given a million holy blessings,
May a new Pope follow his example,
In the coming years,
May the faithful continue to do good works,
In his name, Pope John Paul II,
The sovereign Pope of fortitude,
Of strength, dedication and commitment,
Oh praise Pope John Paul II,
Where the doves of Rome fly with peace,
Long live liberty, freedom and love,
With understanding to all religions,
May the holy church of Rome rejoice,
The Catholic warrior prince,
Who now resides with God in Heaven,
In remembrance a worldly prince has died,
Oh praise him gloriously forever more,
The great Pontiff of Rome,
Ordained to become a saint.

James S Cameron

A MILLION YEARS

Will it take a million years,
Will it take a million tears
To replace hate with love?

Will it take a million years
To understand the reason
Why men sow those seeds of bitterness?

Will it take a million years
To forgive what has happened in the past?
Protestant or Catholic
What difference does it make?

Will it take a million years
To forgive the past and remember
We were all made in God's image?

Julia Holden

UNTITLED

In the eye does beauty hold,
Beauty warm or beauty cold?
Beauty in the endless mile,
A half-baked selfless subtle smile.

Beauty in the claws of death,
The fallen soldier's last drawn breath,
Dark in standing, light in grace,
Is beauty in a hidden place?

Paul Roberts

INVASION

He was invaded
Without hostility or violence,
By a silent adversary, - *walking*
Hand in hand with ticking time
Through the recent months and years,
To inhabit his consciousness.

His lodged opponent
Is a master of psychology,
Empowered with the memory of -
Her presence - exciting and elating,
Her voice, her smile and warm embrace -
To conquer his normality.

Once a visitor
Now a permanent companion
Adored - yet increasingly intrusive,
She eclipses his everyday thoughts.
Diary dates mark future meetings,
Preceding time gnaws at his stomach.

Disturbed and dismayed
His tidy life is destabilised.
The smiling tormentor reveals nothing.
Emotional intricacies sting like acid.
This should not be happening!
His defence must be love - love for his wife!

Robbie Ellis

BYE HOPE

(22/10/99-30/4/00)

You are now free now free of pain
an angel floating on her way
I hope you loved the time you had
take some happy memories with you

you never got to the swings or slide
or wore a school uniform
but I was proud of you in different ways
courage is something beyond measure
you showed me how to be brave

the doctors did all they could
but sometimes healing is just beyond reach
God has you now and you are perfectly well
dancing and singing where you belong

thanks for coming into my life
you are in my heart and will always be there
Christmas birthdays you'll always miss them
we'll remember you and blow a kiss up to Heaven

I think you were sent to us for a reason
to appreciate all that we have
we have learnt what's important in life.

Mummy x

Karen Wileman

SOME KIND OF HEAVEN
(In memory of Ian Curtis 18.05.80)

Is this some kind of Heaven?
Is this some kind of dream?
I've died to myself
Life is not what it seems
Is this some kind of Hell?
Is this some kind of prison?
A new religion, can't make a decision
Is this some kind of Heaven?
Is this reality?
I'm tired and bored of this locality
Is this some kind of Heaven
Or is it some kind of Hell?
That last fatal hour is nearing
As Satan rings the bells
One last cigarette
One last kiss
Give me the rope
Fall into the abyss
I can see a bright light
I can see the Earth
I can see the gates of Heaven
I can see the birth of man
This is where I now belong
This is where I'll stay
Heaven is a paradise
Where every day is a beautiful day
I've finally broken free
Of a life of deceit and lies
I've gone to meet my maker
I have truly died.

A P Richardson

No Answers

I guess nothing ever was the way
I thought it was
And now the fire in your eyes
Has burnt part of my heart away
And now I'm in ashes
I have been exchanged
Mistaken for my body and face
Betrayed by pretty words they all say
A tourist in my life
Crying tears that won't dry
Laughing at empty walls
Praying to the indigo sky
Hoping God has time to listen
Cursing my life
Wanting
Pushing away
Fighting
Giving up
Needing all your love
Needing all your hate
And needing nothing
And all of this just the same
Word full
Word less
Alone
Not alone
With you
Without you
Holding on
Letting go
And then comes the point
Of whatever for
And no answers coming
Till I don't look for them.

Petra Whiteley

ONE LIFE

We only have one life to live,
With which, to do our best.
Hopeful that, at the end,
We will have passed the test!

Every day, brings something new,
If we keep an open mind.
Knowledge, is a gift to share,
It's there for all mankind.

All our planet's treasures,
Should be, for everyone,
Every creature, on this Earth
Since creation first began.

Follow all your hopes or dreams
With heart and mind for guide.
No matter if you're sometimes wrong,
At least, you will have tried!

To reach old age - frustrated,
With regret for chances wasted,
Is a bitter pill to swallow,
Memories are the life you've tasted!

Years pass by, so quickly,
Our lifespan, is so short,
Use every opportunity,
Experience can't be bought!

Wonders of science, never ceasing,
Nature's beauty, majesty, awe,
Man's amazing, innovations,
Embrace them all, for your memory store!

E M Eagle

I WILL NOT

I will not throw upon the floor
The crusts I cannot eat
For many a little hungry one
Would think it was quite a treat
For wilful waste brings wilful want
And I may live to say
Oh how I wish I had that crust
Which once I'd thrown away.

Griffith H Davies

A NEW DAY DAWNS

On 15th January 2005, my emotions took a dive.
Months of pain and anguish behind me,
Feeling like a wilted tree,
I decided - *no more!*
The time has come to do something for me.
My listener said to me,
When will you love yourself?
Do something for you?
On 15th January 2005,
New year barely started,
New year barely begun,
I took the phone in my hand and yelled,
Chesters here I come!
I went down with trepidation,
My heart was all a-flutter.
Sat down, stomach filled with butterflies.
The stylist began to work her magic.
I watched - sometimes chatting,
Sometimes silent - struck with awe,
Watching the transformation,
That with deft hands she wrought.
When she had finished, my heart leapt for joy.
Looking back at me, was a beautiful stranger.
This could not be me!
I was transfixed, amazed, struck dumb!
Feeling ten years younger, looking ahead,
I knew my journey had begun.
My journey - a new beginning,
A new day dawning.

Rosie Heartland

CATACOMBS

We entered the narrow passageway
Thirty feet or more beneath the surface
The silence, coolness and earthy smell
Marking our entrance into a hallowed place
A labyrinth of galleries stretched before us
Housing the burial chambers of millions
Who had passed away many centuries before.

We continued on our journey
Along the narrow, winding tunnels
Of this strange, intriguing underworld
Our whispers sometimes disturbing
The stillness and repose of these resting places
Tombs now empty with the passing of time.

Centres of devotion and pilgrimage
Down through the centuries
Archives of the primitive church
A message of faith, a Christian testimony,
Evidence of a past life, a turbulent existence
Forever lost in the shimmering shadows of time.

An age later . . . we emerged
From the chill and the darkness
Into the bright light of day
Warm sunshine invigorating our senses
Reawakening our zest for living.

Liam Heaney

THE DIET

Everyone was in agreement as we were all too fat
So my wife decided she would do something about that
We'd go and see a hypnotist, that's just what we would do
Our friends Jackie and Mary said they were coming too

She booked it for the Wednesday and she was all excited
'What about Jackie and Mary, do they know you've decided?'
'Oh yes,' she said, 'that they do and they can't wait for it.'
So I glanced up at the ceiling and then I thought a bit.

In the end I did agree it wouldn't do us any harm
Then she fluttered her eyelids and gently took my arm
'You know it won't my dear; it's bound to do you good
You know that you should cut down on your intake of food.'

So I went into the bathroom and stepped upon the scales
Yuk! Fifteen stone seven pounds with no top hat or tails
I pulled my stomach in but the scales they read the same
And I finally resigned myself to play her silly game

Our friends turned up, Jackie smiled and then he looked aloft
'What a load of silly nonsense,' I whispered really soft
Then we all got in the car and were chatting happily
And Mary said I was so strong it wouldn't fizz on me.

I smiled a reassuring smile and smugly thought, *she's right*
I glanced around the others, *would they succumb tonight?*
When we arrived he ushered us in and we soon settled down
'You are going to sleep,' he said and I thought, *what a clown!*

My eyes became so heavy and his voice was fading so
The others started roaring with laughter at what I didn't know
'Jim's snoring,' Mary sniggered, I could hear her in my dream
When I came to I was all alone, this man was really keen

'You are an excellent subject,' I was shocked to hear him say
The others? They were still giggling about fifteen feet away
We left and I was still bemused, and then Mary said, 'Where to?'
'What about fish and chips?' I said, and they said, 'That'll do!'

Jim Bryans

MIDDLE-AGED LADY?

She calls herself 'middle-aged lady'
Which really is hard to believe,
But maybe she finds it amusing
To rag, or to tease or deceive?

No stone is unturned for perfection,
Her visitors treated with care -
The couch is tried here, 'No, it's far better there
But then how do we get up the stair?'

With gusto, this 'middle-aged lady'
Digs on in the garden till dusk;
And she climbs on a wobbly ladder
For sloes to make gin, she collects in a tin,
Though the wind blows in violent gusts.

In the kitchen, this versatile lady
Makes gin from the purple-skinned sloes
After pricking each one as we sat in the sun,
'But how many?' Nobody knows.

In the rain she goes picking blackberries,
She sets out in the car to exchange
Clothes that don't fit, or the colours won't mix,
Or some chairs that refuse to arrange.

She makes wonderful plans for the future
When her home will be buzzing with guests,
Their joy her delight, both by day and by night
So their visit will be of the best.

Her energy really is boundless,
She plans super treats for her guests,
And picnics in heavenly places
For walking and dreaming and rests.

Though she calls herself 'middle-aged lady'
We simply refuse to believe.
'How can it be true, when so much that we do
Is such fun, we're reluctant to leave?'

Nancie Cator

CRAVING

I looked at the shelf,
I'll have twenty of those
It's said they can kill,
Must be true, I suppose!
The price is quite high,
Just to set it on fire.
This little white stick,
To which we aspire!
Spare a thought for the rest,
As the fumes make some choke.
The craving's reduced,
While it goes up in smoke!
The smell lingers on,
Though the smokers can't tell.
To others of course,
It's distasteful as hell!
But rather ironic,
How we spend our cash,
At the end of the day,
There's nothing but ash!
The choice is quite simple,
We can just carry on,
But remember our friends,
The ones - that are gone!

T G Bloodworth

EMERALD ISLE

A glittering emerald isle juts out,
looks like a teddy bear.
The people living on the isle,
all know it, call it Eire.
A little chunk is missing
the back of teddy's head.
Taken over by another land,
poor Eire, nearly dead.

How can any land or thing
live without a brain?
This little part of teddy's head
has made us all insane.
Many dead, for teddy's head
what's the point, we ask?
There is no answer
'tis so ingrained.
The mold is firmly cast.

So how to help poor teddy?
It's taken years to ask.
Even now, his brains spill out,
the sacrificial cow.
They wonder how to fix this,
it's obvious to me.
Just get it back together
all live in harmony.

Rochelle Moore

ICE CREAM MADNESS

(To children everywhere)

Microchip computers are the wonder of the age
Children they can use them, cell phones are all the rage
But when an ice cream van appears, as when I was a child
Technology goes down the drain, the children still go wild

The ice cream van that has *Oor Wullie* painted on the side
Plays a jolly tune for little smiles to open wide
Rebecca and her little chum, run home to money get
To buy ice cream it's on your mark and for a treat get set

I walked along the street one night, the ice cream van had stopped
Heather and wee Alan Dumpling, to its counter hopped
With a bunch of ice cream cones, they rushed back full of glee
Shouting thank you to the man, it raised such joy in me

Fifty years ago I was a child and felt the same
Pleading for some money, when'er the van it came
Palombo or Gallone's 'twas all the same to me
A pokie hat or slider, a tanner was the fee

When just a child we had no TV, just a radio
To the pictures twice a week, we really liked the show
The magic ice cream van was king, a timeless treat it gave
For children haven't changed one bit, 'tis here we end the page.

Roy A Millar

CLIMATIC CHANT

Gust buffets
Drop a wind-wall,
Stall my step,
Whisk away my packet.

Eileen Ellis-Whitfield

GRAVITY

Time for us to see
The static that
Spark our wounds

The distant behind
And the ever after
Is yet to see today.

Turn around, here is the mirror.
See the eye of the storm.
The future unborn, the past cremated

Stand up
You have the power
To pull the gravity of now

Look into the vibration
The tension of your frustration
You'll surely realise
The silence must be spoken.

Christopher Edwin David

ALONE

I was once alone
Now I am not
It is only me and a friend
Who is alone not me
Alone with my voices
Alone with my friend
More and more I seek the truth
To be alone and not really there
To be alone and not really here
Alone with my friend
Alone with my thoughts
That is alone.

Bob Lewis

GOD'S COUNTRY

Heading south from Schiehallion, down to Kenmore
where Ben Lawers overlooks the loch's northern shore
it's a national nature reserve today!

Entering Loch Dochart, better known as the Fillan
the name changes from Dochart to Loch Tay at Killin
where it's now a river, wending its way

into dark, swirling water, now in full spate
spanned by a five arched bridge, built by General Wade,
near the Falls O'Moness, at the Birks O'Aberfeldy.

Heading north to the Soldier's Leap, near Loch Faskally, dark and deep
two rivers run now, to Logierait, where fast flowing Tummel and Tay
both meet,
the local churchyard houses three mort-safes, prevents dead
bodies being carried away.

Almost halfway, to the city of Perth
cross the river to Birnham,
where Beatrix Potter to stories gave birth,
deep in the woods of birch and oak,
where once it moved in a Shakespearean play.

Hunting Tower, Scone Palace, a polder of Scotland history
the whereabouts of that crowning stone, is still quite a mystery!
This is the home of our fighting battalion always ready, night and day.

Now we're on the penultimate run, passing Newburgh and the village
of Errol,
it's in about here they found the Cairncross pearl,
once famous for its salmon grounds; now only the Firth of Tay.

It's been a gae long haul to the city by the sea
the watter an' miles tae bonnie Dundee!
'Ae cam fae Dundee,' as MacGonigal would say.

James Fraser

RESCUED

A rose-bud,
saddened by
harsh autumn rain
stands proud in a
waisted cutglass
gradually revealing
her delicate secrets.

Godfrey Dodds

THIS WORLD OF OURS

Whatever has happened to this world of ours
so many a rebel without a cause
where is the gent who once tipped his hat
or the child who asked, 'Please may I help you with that?'

Where is the young man who graciously gave up his seat
or the people who smiled as you passed on the street
faces now sad . . . they never smile as before
old people now prisoners behind a locked door.

You don't stroll through the woods for fear of attack
youths roam the streets not in groups now but packs
you never carry a purse, why, that's easy to snatch
and several large bolts now replace the door latch.

You're not safe on the bus . . . at least not at night
you're sure to witness some terrible fight
there is dirt and graffiti all over the seat
and marks where somebody has wiped their feet.

You stay at home and you switch on TV
there is violence and crime, little else to see
so you go to bed and simply can't win
you don't really rest, someone may break in.

You make a fresh cup of tea, it could be a long night
you sit in the dark and you shiver with fright
wrapped up in a blanket to keep in the heat
electricity too dear . . . the bills you can't meet.

For I am an old aged pensioner you see
and life is not easy for the likes of me
oh I have a choice, it was given quite free
an old people's home or my dignity.

Doreen Pankhurst

THIS SHORT LIFE

Seventy years or just a day,
We are not really made to stay.

If all is well, we wish to go on,
But in pain we'd rather go, than moan.

To live forever as beauty's child,
Is everyone's dream, the mild as the wild.

The child who dies, does not know,
The glory and suffering of life on the go.

She has barely left the womb, and goes right back,
To be born again, elsewhere, right on track.

When it is time for me to go,
I hope dying is fast, although life was slow.

Alan Bruce Thompson

CREATIVE WRITING

When I write,
Suddenly everything I hear or see,
Takes on a special meaning just for me,
Then I change,
And the person I become,
Forgets everything including being a mum,
Sometimes I go temporarily mad,
Talk to the wall, or get really sad,
Then as suggested by my mentor,
I begin to look slightly left of centre,
And start to think,
What if,
He got really cross,
And murdered his boss,
Or she lost her mother,
And found a brother,
Then,
The space that was so blank and white,
Disappears as I start to write,
And I am lost.

Sally Ann Boardman

AGONY

At this moment I wish we had never met.
The pain I feel is too much to bear and yet.
I know it will pass and I'll feel whole once more.
But our lives will not be as they were before.
Why did I give in and let you have your way?
One day soon I'm going to make you pay.
For the fear and pain you are putting me through.
How could I have thought I was in love with you?
I want to scream, I want you out of my life.
But don't you dare go, I need you I'm your wife.
Your platitudes don't help, it's your fault not mine.
Don't tell me when it's all over I'll be fine.
I'm in agony and all you do is smile.
It's me not you that travels the final mile.
But now I hold him and all I feel is joy.
The pain has gone and we have our baby boy.

Ann Blair

GRANNY

I never knew my granny
which makes me rather sad,
but if I had I'm sure that
I'd recall the fun we'd had.
I'm sure she would have
baked the bestest
cake in all the world,
and told me stories
and taught me to dance
as round and round, we twirled.
I'm sure that she'd have
sung to me
and whispered secrets, too.
I'm sure that she'd have
whispered that she loved me,
loved me true.
I'm sure that we'd go shopping,
and walking in the park,
that she would wipe my
tears away; protect me
from the dark.
I never knew my granny
but I'm sure she'd be the best,
and wherever Granny
might be now,
I'm certain she's at rest.
The only thing I'd like to say
is thank you from my heart,
for I'm the granny now
and I know just where to start.
I'll whisper songs
and make up tales,
and bake the bestest bread,
and tell my grandson
all about the pictures
in my head.

But more than this,
I know I'll tell him,
'Andrew, I love you,'
And keep him safe within my heart
as I know my gran would do!

J P Henderson-Long

BEELZEBUB

Old BB came down to my town
He knew of rich pickings there,
With his sallow skin, his evil eyes
And his oily, greased down hair.
I don't know if I was his first,
But he approached me in the street,
And offered me some easy money
And well, I got to eat.
Well old BB became my friend that day,
Always faithful to his word,
But something about him struck me
He smelt like a fresh, ripe turd.
He was always pretty pushy,
He pushed me to a problem or two,
And whenever I was doing wrong
He stuck to me like glue.
But one day I met a lady
She was as sweet as honeydew
And it wasn't long before we were in love,
Just a day or two.
From then on there were changes
And old BB got the hump,
Because my sweet girl
She turned him around
And kicked him up the rump.
Well from that day on, old BB
Has kept out of my life
Although it's taken a kick or two
From my sweet, darling wife.

Albert Keith Still

ALL CHANGE

New Year approaches, oh what will I do?
Plan new changes, or carry on the same?
Better get moving, it's just a whisper away
Then it will be New Year's Day.

What a bad year, was this last year.
So much sadness, so much pain.
Never want another like that,
Have to be ready for what is to come,
But how is that possible - surely you cannot?

Please, please let it be good.
Oh, how I long for more good news,
Seeking new and exciting challenges,
Not holding back, and ever optimistic.

Miriam Reid

MR BLAIR AND MR BROWN

When Mr Blair met Mr Brown
He ordered a five course lunch
Then sent the bill to the public
And they said thanks a bunch.
I've told more lies than Errol Flynn
About so many things
I ought to be in pictures
With a halo and silver wings.

Parrott and Straw have just gone out
With tin hat, bucket and spade
They have gone to repel the invasion
Of lies that the Labour have made
And all with a bucket and spade.
Now about this immigration
I'd say about six million more
To help out Margaret Beckett
When she starts scrubbing the floor.

I could never make my mind up
About what I'd like to be
I'll try for a sweeper upper
Down at the BBC.
Gordon, I've got the very job
That you want at No. 10
I need a good toilet flusher
You flush to the chimes of Big Ben.

You could flush away all my secrets
Though some might be betting slips
I've got four million with Ladbrookes
I'll be buying Michael Howard fish and chips.
There's rumours of another dome
With Falconer with a spade
Digging up all the dirt and deceit
That Campbell and Hoon have made.

And what about David Kelly
Who should be with us today
Instead of the scum at No. 10
We have to put up with today.

Ian Proctor

BLACK HALF

It's dark in here,
No light
But everyone passes through at least once,
No hope for those who have already fallen.

Fireflies buzz around my head like a luminous halo lighting my path.
I can see now,
A path that leads out from the dark!

The pebbled path!
Like a scorned backbone of the one that has fallen,
It lies here as a reminder of the fate of a pessimist.

Looking down I see, and feel
Like a flashback in a dream,
My bones, my identity part of this path
And others walk among them.

I'm taking my first step!
On this new path, the path of the living.

Out of the cave into the light.
I don't look back . . .

Steven Thurlow

MY POETRY

Here is my poetry, for what it is worth.
A pillar of heartbreak: a puddle of mirth.
A cross between Byron and Donald Duck -
This is my poetry - such is my luck!

Gol McAdam

UNTITLED

The unknown beckons
And draws me forward.
An invisible cord
Tied tight and sure
Pulls gently at my essence
And I know that it is time
To go.

A light glows dimly -
Growing as I approach.
Slowly but surely
Swallowing the path.
I clutch my one way ticket
And resist looking back.
Time stops.

The doorway shines
A brilliant white.
My eyes grow wide
Then fill with anticipation.
A distant hand reaches
And its touch is warm.
I yield.

In whispers and flashes
My memories are exhibited.
A smile curves
And a tear drops
With a resounding echo
But perfect elegance.
They call.

My last glimpse
Is deliberately measured
As the world is veiled.
Satisfied and weary
I dry my eyes
And hold out my hand to wave
Goodbye.

Hannah Pay

LOVE IS FREE

There sat in a little box
A heart not seen or heard
The box had a rose, a card
A phrase to be read
The box was given as a present
A daughter found her heart
Turned and kissed her mother
They smiled at each other
It was a belated Christmas present
Given in February 2005
At Christmas it was not thought of
Forgotten; because her mother's cousin died
Her daughter kissed her mother's cheek
She loved her present
Mother sensed her daughter's heart
Love showed towards the other
Presents find hearts
They cost nothing . . .
For love is an emotion
That is free -
The box was empty
Void except a heart
A heart that could only be found
With love.
Anyone can find love
If they have a heart so true
Mother now goes to sleep
Knowing her daughter loves her too.

Josie Lawson

WHY?

As the unicorn cries
and the waterfalls drop their tears,
the sun lowers its heart
as the clouds drift apart.
Darkness falls,
no happiness in this land
as the stars and galaxies
sparkle onto the Earth's lands
and asks why so many
wars on your land?
Earth spins and nods
I don't know why,
do you know the reason why?

David Turner

New Beginnings?

It looked like a new beginning
Like focusing weary eyes into a kaleidoscope,
Beautiful visions drawing me in;
A sudden influx of positive feelings
So estranged, I'm unable to name them.

Yet this remains

The magnetism of the ocean
Where I return endlessly.
Releasing pent-up inner emotion.
Until I'm spent.

Still watching, the light on the water dances
Transferring my thoughts to trances
And I'm driftwood again,
Immersed and seeming new.

But out of the water I dry.
Sun-bleached.
Parched.
Eroded by the incessant motion
Of harrowing ocean waves.

Lorraine Burden

EXPLODE

Found the end of my rainbow
On the brow of a mystical hill
Shifting twilight on my window of life
Brighter stars in angels' sight

Talking eyes, no words to relate
With equal mind a magical fate
Straight to the core, entwining extreme
Unfolding pleasure's perfect dream

Beauty unravelled a brittle heart
Injected romance with perfect art
Releasing streams that never flowed
Passion, devotion, affection explode.

R S Wayne Hughes

PROBLEM SOLVED

The boss came up to me and said,
'It's time for you to leave,
You've served us well for fifty years
But now you're old, so off you go.'
That is what he said.
A handshake
Not a golden one I fear,
Goodbye old chap
What was the name again?
Then in a nearby hostelry
A jar or two with special friends
Thus the daily treadmill ends.
Now what am I to do
Slump in a chair and watch TV
And slowly rot away,
That's not for me.
I'll get some hardboard, brushes too
And paint a masterpiece or two
But that's no good
The loft's too small to store
Useless works of art galore
Travel?
I did that in the war
But now the world's a violent place
Full of rebel gangs
Out on another killing spree,
And anyway
'This scepte'd isle'
Is good enough for me.

G R Bell

Too Soon

The sun's horizon, splits yellow through blue,
Orange and red the depths in you.
A fish you caught in a boat for two,
But alone on the sea are my thoughts of you.

The wind carried your ashes atop the white horses,
And down into a sea of blue.

Earthly spirit in a land of green,
Your red hair a mark of me.

The father, the sun, in all of you,
With wit and humour we remember you.

Darren Cronin

DREAMING

The dream was water, the dream was steam
The dream was troubled, the dream was serene
The dream was short, the dream was long
It acted in mime then sang a sweet song
The dream was violent, the dream was calm
It lacerated the soul then applied healing balm
The dream was a square, the dream was a cube
The dream was a spiv, the dream was a rube
The dream was fuzzy, the dream was clear
The dream was teetotal, the dream liked its beer
The dream had a punch like the kick of a mule
The dream was a sage, the dream was a fool
The dream was jack-in-the-box
Paradox on the rocks, knitting socks
Picking locks, stirring woks
Hunting fox, winding clocks
Down by the docks, watching ships
Making trips, with flags unfurled round the world
The dream was without beginning or end
It carried straight on and went round the bend
The dream was even, the dream was odd
The dream was the Devil fencing with God
The dream was the first cry and the last breath
The dream was the big bang and entropic death.

Philip Corbishley

THE ANSWER

If we all join in prayer to have world peace
with no rancour to breed its discontent,
then violence and treachery would cease

so we'd have little need of our police
(except for thieves or traffic incident)
if we all join in prayer to have world peace.

With terrorists' actions on the increase,
prayer seems the only way to implement
that violence and treachery will cease.

Whilst recognising life is just on lease,
lost by old age, illness or accident,
if we all join in prayer to have world peace,

intensely, with the might of elbow grease
and bond of international cement,
then violence and treachery would cease.

Oh just to see that worldwide press release
praising the power of prayer's accomplishment!
If we all join in prayer to have world peace
then violence and treachery would cease.

Joy Saunders

RHAPSODY IN TWO!

The butterflies are now fairies
Goldfish swim in a handy stream
Although the dish does now seem empty
One still can taste the cream
Moonbeams on high are gaily dancing
To the harmony of a sweet refrain
Even flowers seem more entrancing
For there is happiness again
The whole world for them is singing
A stupendous joy abounds
O'er the hills those two are winging
A great appreciation of sounds
Now there be a heavenly chorus
A choir now sings in harmony
We all gaze on the vision before us
We all knew that it had to be
For so long they were distressed
Now this association will be blessed
A dad, a mother - grandparents too
A great 'family' feeling is born anew
He is one who cherished dearly
Now this is right we can see that clearly
They had admired each other's charms
Now enwrapped in each other's arms
For so long a passion test
We prayed that he'd not have an 'arrest'
Two old 'fogies' they were to we
But young in heart as we now see
Two old folk from partners parted
Who for years, had been broken hearted
They'll enjoy life with He above
Our old relatives so much in love.

Jon 'El' Wright

DARK ANGEL

Dark angel, fallen from grace.
Hidden within the night.
Beauty not evil hides in lace.
Dejected from above
Because of beauty so great
Only compared to a fresh rose
As precious as a petal
Sharp as a thorn
Stunning just the same
Pure of heart
Right of mind
Just kicked out of Heaven
Door slammed behind.

David Maguire

THEN AND NOW

Now they don't sit down for meals,
Of meat and two vegetables.
Talk with their friends, feel comfortable
Instead school children jostle about the shops,
Buy handfuls of sweets,
Walnut whips,
Battered pancakes with chips.

They don't even taste junk dishes,
Of the children of the fifties.
Ham, Spam, bread and jam,
Six of bread and dripping.
Once a week boiled fish.
Did not crave for sweets,
Walnut whips, things with chips.

Then daily third of pint of milk
At school a welcome drink.
Dinner a wholesome meal,
Sat down with friends,
Did not eat dishes that made one obese.
After war dishes,
Kept one quiet.

George B Clarke

UPON THIS SACRED GROUND

For a heavenly feeling
Some do not believe
In expanding your mind
Secrets to the universe
You can find.

Whatever it may be
On brown or proverbial 'E'
None of this helps me
Or those that surround
Upon this sacred ground

The world is opening up
Drinking from the knowledge cup

Enter the fountain of belief
Faith returns, what a relief
So sad to lose your belief.

Donna Hardie

DEATH

Death is like the end of the day
Like a book turning its last page
Eternal darkness.
Rest!

Andy Wheeler

A Letter To My Inner Child

I know you're there somewhere
Hiding deep out of sight
I know I've neglected to love you
But I will make things right
I know I've not attempted to play
Or join in your games
I know for years, I've ignored you
And I'm deeply ashamed
I know you probably don't like me
For those things that I've done
But please come out of the shadows
And walk with me in the sun.

Come here little Carl
And take told my hand
There's nothing more to fear,
If together we stand.

Carl Thurston

REJECTION

Woke up in the stark, winter night,
could not feel my own body,
felt as I was outside seeing myself,
it wasn't a pretty sight, wondered if my time had come.
Wished the phone would ring,
but I had neglected my friends
and no one rang anymore.
Got the car out and drove slowly, like a drunk,
to the hospital, waiting room full of sick humanity,
got a number and waited. Must have slept.
When I awoke the ailing were still there
Nothing had moved except the clock on the wall
and it was morning.
Went to the café, had a coffee and a bun
drove home, death had rejected me
And that was OK as it looked to be a fine day.

Jan Oskar Hansen

SOUTHERN ROADS

I guess we tread the boards with secret loads
and learn, alone, how young stuff quickly goes
like friends, alive or dead on rocky roads.

You didn't see my jilted life of rides
but watched across some carriageway, and knew
the rest could tread my boards with empty loads.

The rest had riddled love in sloppy raids
on dreaming, studied shires, but I am through
with friends acquired or lost on risky roads.

I've written twenty years of lousy reads
and lost that southern thing to be with you,
while others left my life with stolen loads.

You tell me that the past is where we lied
while I discover futures that remove
the friends who shut or shaped my rutted roads.

Forgive me when the drudgery implodes -
you are the only one to love and know.
I guess we tread the boards with secret loads
while friends should live or die on separate roads.

Will Daunt

DARK SACRED NIGHT

It was always hard to touch you
Believing my love was wrong
As naiveté changes to virtue
An armour of fear is gone.

Reborn into nakedness
It's pleasure to lie by your side
In a birthday suit of innocence
There is freedom in nothing to hide.

So wrap me up in your softness
Melt away all the fear
I realise that you love me
If not, I would not be here.

There is an ocean in your breathing
Creation of life in your words
Cover me with your fragrance
Cushion me in your pearls.

Let me blend with your darkness
Cocooned in the velvet of night
Star maps of the heavens
Are witnessed to my flight.

Mano Warren

WAITING

They stand like sentinels the ivy-clad trees,
Waiting leafless in their 'fancy dress',
Waiting for summer's sun to caress
Their twisted limbs,
Hopefully spring will once again bless
Their budless twigs.
A carpet of colour below,
As bluebells bloom where once lay a blanket of snow,
Swaying branches in a wind
Sometimes toppled by a gale.
Lightning may split and fire consume,
But still they wait, while we grow frail,
Some perhaps were here before you or I,
And may well be standing,
Patiently waiting to shade our resting place,
When comes *our* time to die.

Christine May Turner

DEPARTURE FOR BUCHENWALD

The platform throngs with humour,
Doors are slammed with goodwill,
The lovers are lacking in glamour
But they are happy and hopeful; they thrill

To this moment of joy,
The supreme perhaps of their lives,
When goodness is voiced unalloyed,
And no dark future deprives them

Of wholesome and genuine bliss.
But for others to come, departure is dire:
Hands will reach, lips not kiss,
As they come to their funeral pyre.

How odd; the outstretched hand
Skywards above the crowd,
Is the sign of the lowest band
Of men, which nature has yet endowed.

Yet the hand in a downward way,
Is the hand which longs to care;
Though it innocently drags its love away
To a Hell beyond despair.

James Stevenson

FEELINGS NOT PICTURES

Feel free to carry me when I fall
when all is lost and that all I can presume is
that you've done it . . .

Left.

Side by side and now nothing
not even a call . . . 'How do you do?'
or 'I miss you.'

The language of life is unspoken.
You don't have to tell me!
I see.

Even without the eyes I feel it.
And feelings not words, or pictures
truly hurt.

Angela Fothergill

YOU

You speak
Words of music
Come to me

You smile
My world lights up
For a single moment

You talk
I listen
My happiness hangs on every word

You laugh
It makes me smile
Should I go on?

You are my sunshine
You are the light
In the midst of all the darkness

You guide me
Inspire me
And give me comfort in the lonely days

And even when you look through me
I hope
You feel for me like I do for you
But I know the truth
I just can't face it.

Kirsty Gillespie (14)

FLAME

Ships that move into the night
Like my nerves of distant dance
Searching comfort to hold me close
She left me for another chance

My eyes are drawn in the naked flame
The flickering light casts its spell
To draw me to the flames' desire
To search again for my heart that fell

My mind is lost to catch a dream
To bring her back to hold again
But from this space she melts away
Back to a world with other men

I lay my head to escape the cage
To slip away and find some peace
To rest the hurt of a breaking child
Only to drift away with no release

My dreams are wild of being chased
Of creatures large with eyes of red
I'm running fast to escape my fate
To wake with sweat on a lonely bed

I'm back again to find a life
To draw again from a place that knows
To give me purpose and desire
From the calling graves in waiting rows

Ricky N Lock

BLACK ANTS

A black army
Marching calmly
Across the floor,
Craving sugar
Or something sweet
To eat.
Unafraid they go,
Headstrong, hell-bent
Searching for what they need
To thrive and keep alive.
Unafraid, they parade.
Are they being clever
Or is instinct their guide?
Making up for size
By being wise,
Owning an army
Of ants galore
Which cross the floor,
And go on for ever
And ever, and ever.

Margaret Nixon

IF LIFE . . .

If life is just a journey,
The world is lost at sea,
The tides are always changing,
Or so it seems to me,

If life is like the water
My friends would be the shore,
We'd depend on the weather,
As we did once before,

If life is just existence,
Then I guess we're not real,
Our blinkered eyes don't really see,
Our scars don't really heal,

If life was a big book,
I would be a wizard,
Everyone would need to look,
When I turn into a blizzard.

L Holt & D Lomas

HEAVEN'S DOOR AJAR

I opened my eyes, looked, then said to myself,
'My world has been changed by a mischievous elf.'
For as I was shopping from frozen food shelf,
Heaven wanted me for God's bargain of wealth.
I'd not found it painful, in fact was quite nice,
Though not sure if I were God's sugar or spice.
Suddenly I realised that people all round
Were struggling to retain me here on the ground.
Ambulance man and lady fighting so hard
To keep on this earth, soul of old woman Barb.
When the end result will be just the same,
Seems such a pity it will all be in vain.
I tried very hard to aid spiritually,
Heard relief in man's voice saying, 'She'll make it, you see.'
Into their vehicle went Barb, whom they took
To just be checked over at hospital Addenbrookes.
After all that as they were letting her home,
A new trick was played by an impudent gnome.
Now I'm a patient in one of their beds,
Shock having frozen the use of my legs.
From then on moved from pillar to post,
Helped on my way by an impudent ghost.
Someone at sometime doing essentials to me,
So much to find out before I'm set free.
That second collapse stopped them letting me go,
How all this happened, I really don't know.
The answer's so simple to blunt folk like me,
It isn't with flowers or an ice cream tea.
I smile at the ghost, I shake hands with my gnome,
The problem be solved if they just send me home.

Barbara Goode

EFFORT

A lick of a stamp and a walk to the post box.
A drive to the shops to replace all those old socks.
Flossing your teeth. All a bore and a chore now.
A badge saying 'Kate's Room' just stuck on her door now.

Watching wet clothes in the heat as they spin round.
Microwave chips signal *done!* in a thin sound.
Turn on the TV. Reality showdown.
Leave your books shut. Mentality slowdown.

Shall I shower now, instead of the morning?
No. One more drink to stifle the yawning.
Think of the things I haven't quite done yet.
Shopping. OK. I'll start up the internet.

Ordering bread with a click on the PC.
Nothing is said. God forbid, you may see me.
Close the door tight. It's night and it's dark out.
World makes you tired. It's best to be spark out.

Geoff Bennett

PICTURE THIS

A crowded bar
Full of noise and smoke.
Wave upon waves of thoughts
Bombarding my brain
Like meteor showers.

A large glass of lager
Gleaming
From the highly polished table.
Wearing a crown of white foam.

In a corner,
An old man sits,
Reading yesterday's
Evening Mail.
His eyes look up,
Then return to the page.

From the tannoy:
'Please make your way
To the cinema,
Where tonight's film
Will begin in five
Minutes.'

Silence descends.
Just a handful of
Seasoned onlookers
Remain, seemingly
Glued to their barstools.

Eleven o'clock, out they pour
Too busy gossiping
About the exploits
Of the villain
To watch where they tread.

Not satisfied with their fill,
They head to the bar again,
That 'one for the road'
Which seems to turn into
Two, or three.

After much deliberation,
Some slightly worse
For that extra half,
They stumble out into
The night.

Show's over now.
Last orders called
Time to go.
The cold night air's calling
'Come again soon, won't you?'

John H Foley

GONE BUT NOT FORGOTTEN

Stone statues cry tears of granite behind
Marble headstones worn with age.
The stems of long dead flowers
Once lovingly arranged
Tell of respects once often paid,
Memories long since erased.

Stone statues cry tears of granite
For those that time has left alone
With no one stopping by
To whisper of a love once known.
All that remains is the date of passing; name unknown
The inscription worn away;
The grass overgrown.

Stone statues cry tears of granite
Because there's no longer someone there
To look after those long since passed
To show that we still care.
But a beautifully manicured resting place
For those who have departed
Is not a measure of the love that lives on in our hearts.

Rachael Ajao

DOWN CLOWN

Down Clown, Clown fell down.
Clown fell down when out of town.
When Clown fell down he pulled a frown,
a frown that worried those in town.

Clown went down with Mr Brown,
Mr Brown from out of town.
Clown and Brown had worn a gown,
a gown they'd bought for half a crown.

The coin belonged to Mr Pink,
so Mr Pink then caused a stink.
He only lent them half a crown
to get those fellows out of town.

Then Mr Pink saw Mr Blue,
Mr Blue knew what to do.
Mr Blue called Mr Black.
Mr Black made Clown come back.

Mr Black then sold the gown
so Clown gave Pink his half a crown.
The gown was sold to Mr Grey,
then Clown and Brown went on their way.

Cadenz Rime

DEFUNCT POEM

I nurtured you and
endowed you with life.
You fed on my thoughts
grew strong from my toil.
Each part of you formed
struggling to be whole.

Dissatisfied then
I ended your life
crumpled your body
and
amongst my other thoughts
your foetal shape
rests stillborn
in the trash.

Alan Triffitt

NEW YEAR

Auld Lang Syne
I sang this year
for all our hopes and dreams
remembered days and troubles past
for a better and good near year

raise up your cups
and wish thee well
and shake this hand o' mine
for a better future
and happy days
we'll sing this Auld Lang Syne

so throw your caution to the wind
and shout a mighty cheer
come in through the open door
friends that we hold dear

so Auld Lang Syne
amongst our friends
some old and some are new
we'll share with you a hearty song
to raise our glasses to.

Margery Rayson

MY LOVE

Softly whispered words of love's potent passion
the warmth of your lips pressed against mine
the beat of your heartbeat in rhythm with mine

Steven Evans

SONNET ON THE BEE

When dawn alights, the world is set a-hum!
Small minions of a captive queen fly hence
To gather sustenance; then back they come
Across the miles, drawn home by unknown sense.

A life of service - bearing young, and food,
No rest 'til fall of twilight, or of rain;
Three thousand strong, yet work in solitude . . .
We may believe a bee's life most mundane.

And yet, where beauty blooms, there they are found!
The sweetest nectars of the spring they sip;
In their staunch loyalty, our hopes profound,
That we may emulate their bretherenship,

And in their death - by stinging, paying that price,
We come to understand self-sacrifice.

Leonard Low

IN MOTION

Bitter. Bitter sweet. Sweet.
Head. Torso. Feet.
Red. Yellow. Blue.
Me. Them. You?

Regress. Stillness. Progress.
Peace. Noise. A bloody mess.

Derek Holder

THE FINANCIAL TIMES

Subject to status the advert reads
If your status is right we'll fulfil your needs
Human beings need not apply
It's your bank balance darling, not your reasons why

Subject to status nothing else will do
Not your heart or your soul or the things you've been through
Not the love you once had, you may even be sad
But what matters my boy, is the house that you have.

Andrew Heywood

SPIRIT OF NEW YEAR

In such silence the crowds await, when
The moment arrives with chimes of Big Ben
Commencing the time of New Year's Day
And so many fireworks on display
Lighting up the dark night sky
In all directions colour does fly
A show of patterns, all shape and size
Forming a bright and colourful disguise
To the midnight atmosphere
All so close and very near
Sounds adding more to the show
And rays of light continue to glow
Crowds of viewers welcome in
A start to a new year, determined to win
All the scenes on show above call
Reflecting from water by the wall
Of the river through the way
finding its route with no delay
Keeping the thoughts in mind for each day
The spirit of new year, cannot go away

James Stephen Thompson

I'LL SCREAM

If another person tells me how lucky I am I will scream
Because I'm coping - but things are not what they seem
I'm in a hole that nothing can fill
The feeling of always going up hill
Yes I am healthy, coping quite well
But for me it's a living hell

You're so lucky - the family is close by
Yes they are, but they can't replace my guy
When you have had 45 years of love and content
It comes as a shock and a very big dent
I miss the laughter and chats in bed
And all the funny things he did and said

If another person tells me how lucky I am - I will scream
He was my best friend - we were a team
It only happens like that - once in your life
And I enjoyed being his wife
I don't understand why - it's just a bad dream
Please don't say I'm lucky - I'll scream

Once more I climb and reach the crown of this hill
Where I can reflect, and be still
I think of all my yesterdays
As I peer through the clearing haze
A rainbow arch stares at me from the sky.
My sorrow somehow says goodbye
With the family's love all around
Happy memories - peace I have found
I am lucky - meet me when I dream
I no longer want to scream

Adeline Reidy

BEDSITTER

Waiting in a seedy little bedsitter in nowhere land
lost beneath a crumpled layer of takeaways and tea
hiding all the tell-tale signs of tedium, monotony
let's revamp the 'femme fatale', the girl you want to see

Putting on a brighter face, the key goes in the latch again
haven't learnt my lesson yet, still breaking every rule
wish I'd got the guts to say I cannot stand this emptiness
look how infidelity has played me for a fool

Somehow can't help thinking how it used to be so simple once
I was kind of 'happy' in a self-destructive way
now I've put the rosy specs to rest for good, regrettably
no point reminiscing on the things we used to say

Never was a one to come to terms with empty promises
all those times I sympathised about your wretched wife
wonder why I gave up being married, in suburbia
wonder what I'm doing here with less than half a life?

Kathryn Atkin

THE DISPOSAL OF MEMORY

Its white, reflection of flesh,
only dismissible and disposable,
tightness betrays thought, and
the flakes of memory penetrate.

The evening's castle retracts
all attention to the night,
the haunting of governing voices in unison.

The guild, swearing occupation and salvation,
fishing in the talents of everyday spectators,
and sightless reward.

Punishment for the dead, for
they don't owe anything,
they are everything,
let's curse them and reward them
with modernist collectivism.

Is it that we are trying to say something?
Let's burn our conceptions of trade
and the everyday,
the void we fill, eyes closed
and mouths open, sound
is lost,
and the horizon is filled with paper excuses,
don't give up, for this was a pointless endeavour
and will be at the disposal of memory,
if it ever gets that far.

Tom Collin

SOMETHING LOVE RELATED

Whisper softly, your dreams of love,
Sweep me up in your tidal wave:
Carry me with you wherever you go,
I want to be there, holding your hand.

Of all that surrounds me, you're the truth:
The only thing that fits with me.
I want to tell you, that I mean it all:
All that's in those words, all that's in those looks.

I want to wrap myself up tight in your arms,
Feel the warmth of your breath upon my skin.
Time seems to stop when it's just you and me:
Our world is untouchable, unstoppable perhaps.

So whisper softly, your dreams of love,
Thread me through them, meet me in them.
Together we can make the voyage,
Holding hands as the world stands still.

Alexa Crawford

NEW BEGINNINGS

I am still surprised I did it
Do you know exactly what *freedom* really feels like?

It's wonderful,
    It's exhilarating,
        It's sometimes and *only* sometimes scary.

It's like trying to walk, talk and run as a small child
You stumble in places
You learn by your mistakes

You try to *exorcise* your past
But
Unfortunately in your dreams your previous life comes back to
Haunt you

The things he did to you
The things you endured
The things that now restrict you

You know it would have been easier if *he* had been taken
Out of the equation and *died*
That was my only way of *salvation*
But strength, wisdom and belief helped me through
And, I did it

I left with my children and I started again

It's three years today I got my *divorce*
I have my piece of paper of *qualified freedom*
And now I am in control, not *him*
I do what I want, when I want, no restrictions,
No rules, no mind games

I have my confidence *back*
I have my self-esteem *back*
I have my self-respect *back*

New beginnings, yes, *welcome back, me.*

Nia Michael

ANOTHER YEAR

Another year has started
Resolutions have been made
Where did the last year go?
Why do I feel afraid?

It's not that I mind getting old
With age I know I'll cope
The year ahead awaits us now
Let's enter it with hope

With faith in God
And lots of love
The way to go is clear
Another chance to live with God, in another year.

Mary Gemmell

JOHN PAUL II

John Paul II has gone to his boss
And the One who went upon the cross
To prepare the Lamb for His return
To aid person-kind good for to learn.

After 'Who Wants To Be A Millionaire?'
Newsflashes told the news
Of John Paul II, 1978 - 2005,
Who worked hard never to skive.

Elected in 1978
When me and Virginia made magic great
Preaching to the whole inhabited Earth
He has earned a second 'birth'.

H Griffiths

THE TIGER STAR

There was a tiger star
That you could see from afar.
The tigers are all around
Eating the food on the ground.
The tigers looked up to the sky
And the cubs just wondered why.
The tigers lay by the bay
Because they had a tiring day.

Fern Pattinson (8)

SUMMER

Sitting in a field there is no sound
Save the rustle of leaves all around.
A gentle breeze plays softly with tall grasses,
And butterflies dance on every flower.

Busy bees with drowsy hum
Sample every flower till all are done;
Butterflies of every hue - blue, white, copper,
Flutter round my head.

So gently plays the lilting wind
Amongst the leaves so green
That I can hardly bear to go,
But stealthy, leave the scene.

So lovely is that faery place
That rabbits play, and join the race
To be a part of that fair scene
Where all is peaceful and serene.

Diana Price

UNTITLED

A famous saying
You can say
Is live old horse
And you'll get hay
For in a day or two
At the most
Your bale of hay
Is in the post.

First his budgie died
For the want of seed
Then his rabbit died
With nothing to feed
Then the old black cat
Well, it died too
And last to go
Was the wee dog, Boo.

So he phones the Social
On the public phone
With his last ten pence
Which he does own
And he is asked
Does he live alone?
'I do,' he said,
'For my friends have died
And up in Heaven
They do abide
And if you check
I will be bound
For that is where
They can be found.'

A Power

SHOES TALK!

Shoes talk
You know that before you can walk
And you lie in your pram
Looking up at the skies
With a smile on your face
And unfocused eyes,
While, sighing and flapping,
Busily tapping,
Shuffling, bustling,
Scuffling, rustling.
Wearily creaking,
Determinedly squeaking,
Unseen, but still speaking,
The shoes hurry by.

Tina Molli

MORNING AND NIGHT

Linda Marie, sweet Linda Marie
Every morning I hold you
Closer and closer
And every night I hold you tight
So I can look into your eyes,
Your beautiful hazel-brown eyes
And kiss your sweet angel lips,
For your love is so warm and tender
Your love is so soft but strong
Your love is that of an angel
I hope to hold and love
My whole life long.

So please, please, sweet Linda Marie
Please, please don't ever leave me
For if you do
My heart will break in two
And I would surely die,
For your love is so warm and tender,
Your love is so soft but strong,
Your love is that of an angel
I hope to hold and love
My whole life long,
For you, Marie, are the love of my life,
You are my warm and tender loving wife.

Donald John Tye

THOUGHTS

What do you think of
When you first wake?

Do you think of me?

Or do other pictures enter your head
Different scenarios
A significant other?

Have I become an afterthought
A postscript in your life?

Time passes
I think
I feel
I yearn

For you
Drifting away
Different scenarios

I cling -
Should I?

Sandra Spears

TRUE

We all need someone
To talk to in our life
A friend whom we can run
In times of stress

A friend who's always there,
Throughout the years,
A friend we know will care
And take away our fears

A friend who's always near,
Waiting for our call,
To wipe away our tears
And lift us when we fall

A loving friend indeed
One who we can depend
To fulfil our every need

A true friend

Tim Harris

AMBROSIA

I wish away my dreams
Into a far off place of music
Where dancing is a language
Passion is an accent
I stand upon a ledge of ice
My balance holding fast
Enchanted prince awaiting me
With temptation at a glance
Eyes around my body
Circling my every move
How am I to fly again
When chains restrict me
A river of blood beckons me
As the sweet smell of death
Opens my pores
Enticing me forward
With the promise of love
I drift alone in my mind
My dreams a vacant echo
This silken lined vision
Is a rose tinted truth
That holds me forward
When I beg for more

Barbara Fox

WHO ARE THEY?

They said that eggs could harm you
Now they say they won't.

They say that certain diets work
Now they say they don't.

They said it's going to snow next week
Now they say it's not.

They said certain weapons are in Iraq
Now they say that's rot.

I wish *they* would make up their minds
Decide which seeds they're sowing
And then perhaps I could find out
Which way the wind is blowing.

Jill Mackness

MIRRORS

Mirrors that hang on the wall
Almost the size of a ball.
Reflections move from side to side
Some are wide, some that hide
Each frame has a name,
But they each seem the same.
Staring at still life
Like my dead wife.
Corners sharp as a sword
And my face is stored.

Joshua Yates (10)

An Ending

How can you look and not see
the heart that's dying inside of me.
Your indifference fills me with such pain
yet I can't forgive and start again.

We pass in the hallway, momentarily
sharing a house - living separately.
My name never slips lovingly from your tongue
how can I guess where we went wrong?

The eyes that once shone with laughter
burn into my soul, long after
I've left the room. I sob and moan
as you whisper her name on the telephone.

My clothes hang limply on skeletal frame,
as carelessly you wound and maim.
You whistle as you complete each task.
Can't you see me? Feel my pain? Silently I ask.

Did we ever share a smile -
Even for a little while?
With the children grown, I see clearly now.
Did you ever love me? Sometime? Somehow?

Valerie Wyatt

LA SYMPHONIA DE LA PICADORES

Cervantes shouted from the highway, 'Hey!'
The dust storm rose, tall wild grey rose, growing in horizon's line.
Papyrus scrolls talking to the plains, the roaring plains Espana,
ancient and brittle, wise and harsh, the roaring plains Espana.
The riders in black, dusted covered black, ride bulls like they were birds
tame the knights insignificant, let only to watch the herd
pass them by . . . pass them by . . . pass them by.
With their thunder they take away,
with their enormity they retrieve,
with their blackness mass, storm rolling task, ripple the hearts of men.
The bulls rode hard that day.
Covering all of Spain.
No man was left to speak,
When the bulls rode hard that day,
Covering all of Europe.
Great swathes of land cut through.
But riders' symphony in black.
In black and riding true.

Graeme Robbins

NIGHT EYES

A dark deep portal
Owl looking into my window
Yellow, green bright eyes
Shining a tale of nature
Of the wise fools lonely
Looking at me as
Dark clouds move in the
Sullen night sky
Knowing between us
Blinks once, blinks twice
Ruffles feathers and my mind
And then she flew
Taking the night away

John Ball

THE ZEN GUIDE TO EATING OUT

Bright and breezy,
a good place to eat,
light and airy

A hint of strawberry,
old friends to meet,
bright and breezy

A touch of history
on the Sandman's beat,
light and airy

Green leaves of memory,
fragrant and sweet,
bright and breezy

On wings of eternity,
sad world sure to quit,
light and airy

A passing reality
to keep the mind quiet;
Bright and breezy,
light and airy

R N Taber

ARISE!

Sing high little bird
With joy
At the beginning
Of this day
Let all the world
Hear your voice
And so refreshed
May too rejoice

Lyn Sandford

MEANINGS

Breath defying
Death defying
Destiny
The future in me.
Beating of life
The cheating, the strife
No comedy
All joking apart
Love not just in the heart
The soul, the fever
It's hotter than that
Passion
Turning about, scream at me, shout.
Can anyone help me?
What's life all about?
A cold cup of coffee
A storm in the spring
The future is handing me
Many new things.
Company
Two - the new meaning of one
Three is true happiness
Four means the breeding is done
Endings
None of these such exist
Merely fantasy
A lie from you to me
Nothing ends
Life is a circle
And life is a friend.

Michelle Sims

WINDOW 'PAIN'

You look at her
She's lost the will
Her desperation
Bleeds her
Through her tears
You can feel
A pain that burns
Much deeper

And as you stand
And watch awhile
Her eyes they gaze
Straight through you
Bewildered how you've
Become this girl
A passing reflection
In the window.

Naomi Hartnell

INFORMATION

We hope you have enjoyed reading this book - and that you will continue to enjoy it in the coming years.

If you like reading and writing poetry drop us a line, or give us a call, and we'll send you a free information pack.

Alternatively if you would like to order further copies of this book or any of our other titles, then please give us a call or log onto our website at www.forwardpress.co.uk

Poetry Now Information
Remus House
Coltsfoot Drive
Peterborough
PE2 9JX
(01733) 898101